Anti Inflammatory Diet For Beginners

The Complete Meal Plan With Tasty Recipes To Heal Your Immune System, Feel Better And Reduce Inflammation

GRACE MORRIS

Copyright © 2019 By Grace Morris

All rights reserved.

This document is geared towards providing exact and reliable information with regards to the topic and issue covered. The publication is sold with the idea that the publisher is not required to render accounting, officially permitted, or otherwise, qualified services. If advice is necessary, legal or professional, a practiced individual in the profession should be ordered.

From a Declaration of Principles which was accepted and approved equally by a Committee of the American Bar Association and a Committee of Publishers and Associations.

In no way is it legal to reproduce, duplicate, or transmit any part of this document in either electronic means or in printed format. Recording of this publication is strictly prohibited and any storage of this document is not allowed unless with written permission from the publisher. All rights reserved.

The information provided herein is stated to be truthful and consistent, in that any liability, in terms of inattention or otherwise, by any usage or abuse of any policies, processes, or directions contained within is the solitary and utter responsibility of the recipient reader. Under no circumstances will any legal responsibility or blame be held against the publisher for any reparation, damages, or monetary loss due to the information herein, either directly or indirectly.

Respective authors own all copyrights not held by the publisher.

The information herein is offered for informational purposes solely, and is universal as so. The presentation of the information is without contract or any type of guarantee assurance.

The trademarks that are used are without any consent, and the publication of the trademark is without permission or backing by the trademark owner. All trademarks and brands within this book are for clarifying purposes only and are the owned by the owners themselves, not affiliated with this document

Table Of Contents

Introduction 1

    Inflammation 3

Chapter One: What Does An Anti- Inflammatory Diet Do? 6

    What Makes Up An Anti-Inflammatory Diet? 11

    Chronic Inflammation And Diet 17

    Step By Step Instructions To Recognize Anti-Inflammatory Diet 21

    A Food List Of What To Eat On An Anti- Inflammatory Diet....23

Chapter Two: The Benefits Of Anti-Inflammatory Foods.........27

    What Does The Anti-Inflammatory Diet Comprise Of? 27

    Anti-Inflammatory Diets: What Do You Eat? 29

    Advantages Of Omega-3 32

    The Benefits Of Natural Anti Inflammatory These Days 37

Chapter Three: What Can I Do To Reduce Inflammation In My Body? 53

    What Causes Inflammation In The Body And How To Control It? 53

    The Guide To Getting Rid Of Inflammation In Your Body 56

    The Best Diet To Reduce Inflammation In The Body 67

Chapter Four: Classic Signs Of Inflammation 84

Chronic Inflammation 84

How Inflammation Triggers Diabetes - And Anti-Inflammatory Tips To Live By 91

The Inflammation-Diabetes Connection 96

How Might You Reduce Your Level Of Inflammation? 98

Inflammation And Anti-Aging 116

Chapter Five: Foods To Avoid 124

Decrease Inflammation Only By Choosing The Right Natural Food 126

Immune System 127

Diets That Cause Inflammation 127

Diets That Fight Inflammation (And Those That Don't) 133

Mitigating Foods To Add To Your Diet 135

The Anti-Inflammatory Diet: How It Can Protect You From Disease 140

Chapter Six: Dieting Protocol – Meal Plan And Recipes 149

Step By Step Instructions To Meal-Prep Your Week Of Meals: . 150

Conclusion 163

Introduction

Anti-inflammation is the use of a food or treatments that reduces inflammation or swelling.

Anti-inflammatory medications make up a portion of analgesics, curing of pains by reducing inflammatory, rather than narcotics, which influence the focal sensory system to alleviate pain signals to the cerebrum.

The Anti-inflammatory diet is an eating plan intended to counteract or reduce poor quality and continual inflammation, a key hazardous factor in a large classification of medical issues and a few significant diseases. The run of the mill alleviation diet accentuates natural products, vegetables, lean protein, nuts, seeds, and solid fats.

There is no Anti-inflammatory diet, rather, there are diets planned around foods that are believed to reduce inflammation and which avoid foods that irritate the incendiary procedures. Numerous Anti-inflammatory diets are based on consuming whole grains, vegetables, nuts, seeds, fresh vegetables and natural products, wild fish and fish, grass-feed lean turkey and chicken which are thought to help in the body's healing of inflammation. They avoid foods that are thought to trigger inflammation, for example, refined grains, wheat, corn, full-fat dairy, red meat, caffeine, liquor, peanuts, sugar, and absorbed and saturated fats.

The impacts of the anti-inflammatory diet are subtle. There is a development of research that shows a benefit in lessening of continuous ailments, for example, cardiovascular disease, neurodegenerative illnesses, and malignant growths when following a dietary example related with the alleviation diet. Be that as it may, the advantages go beyond the prevention of illnesses. Studies have showed a lessening of side effects related to ceaseless infections. Also, an individual may reduce or stop their dose of drugs prescribed to control side effects identified with provocative conditions and lessen the side effects related with anti-inflammatory experts.

It has likewise been noted that individuals who pursued the alleviation diet expressed they encountered loss of weight, had a rise of vitality, and revealed better mental and emotional wellbeing.

The typical creation of Anti-inflammatory diets is the belief that fewer identification of inflammations are the forerunner as well as inflammation to numerous unending ailments. When evacuated, the body can start healing itself. The philosophical beginning of Anti-inflammatory diets goes back to the first healers from the beginning of time who have worked with foods, herbs, teas and other characteristic solutions that helps the body's very own healing vitality.

Endless ailment — an ailment or ailments that endures over a long period of time and some of the time causes a long-term change in the body.

C-receptive protein (CRP) — a marker of inflammation flowing in the blood that has been proposed as a technique to recognize people in danger of these illnesses.

Flavonoid — alludes to mixes found in natural products, vegetables, and certain drinks that have differing beneficial biochemical and cancer prevention agent effects.

Inflammation

Different foods are utilized in an unexpected way, some increasing inflammation and others reducing it. The motivation behind the alleviation diet is to advance ideal wellbeing and repair by choosing foods that lessen inflammation. In the event that one can effectively control extreme inflammation through normal methods (like through an diet), it lessens one's reliance on anti-inflammatory prescriptions that have undesirable and unfortunate effects and don't address the fundamental issues. While Anti-inflammatory drugs, (for example,

NSAIDs) are a convenient solution to ease occurrences, they at last debilitate the invulnerable mechanism by harming the gastrointestinal tract which assumes a significant job in insusceptible mechanism work.

Inflammation is a restricted response of tissue to damage, regardless of whether brought about by microscopic organisms or viral disease, injury, synthetics, heat or other instances that causes disturbance. The 'disturbance' makes the tissues inside the body discharge numerous substances that causes changes inside the tissues. This perplexing reaction is called inflammation.

Inflammation is displayed by such manifestations that include:

1) Vasodilatation of the close veins bringing about an abundance centralized blood flow

2) Increases in the penetrability of the vessels with spillage of enormous amounts of blood into the interstitial spaces

3) May incorporate coagulating of the blood in the interstitial spaces because of much occurrence of fibrinogen and different proteins spilling from the vessels

4) Relocation of granulocytes and monocytes into the tissue in large amounts

5) Swelling of the tissue cells.

The regular substances discharged from the tissues that result in inflammation are histamine, bradykinin, serotonin, prostaglandins, numerous hormonal substances considered lymphokines that are discharged by sharpened T-cells and different other response consequences of different mechanisms inside the body. A considerable amount of these substances activate the macrophage mechanism, which are conveyed to discard the harmed tissue, yet additionally, which further harm living tissue and cells.

CHAPTER ONE

What Does An Anti- Inflammatory Diet Do?

An Anti-inflammatory diet comprises of foods that lessen inflammatory reactions. This diet includes replacing sugary, refined foods with whole, supplement rich foods. Anti-inflammatory diet likewise contains expanded actions of cancer prevention agents, which are responsive particles in food that reduce the quantity of free radicals. They are atoms in the body that may harm cells and increase the risk of specific infections. Numerous famous weight control plans pursue alleviation standards. For instance, the Mediterranean diet contains fish, whole grains, and fats that are useful for the heart. Research has confirmed that this diet can decrease the effects of inflammation on the cardiovascular framework.

The body's resistant framework is intended to fend off threats, similar to disease causing germs, through a procedure called inflammation. Be that as it may, a relentless bout of inflammation can prompt everything from diabetes to immune system infections, to coronary illness, and to malignancy.

Large amounts of these wellbeing risks don't originate from remote intruders like terrifying microscopic organisms, yet from some ordinary foods you're most likely eating. Removing inflammation inciting foods from your diet, or if nothing else restricting them, can enable you to make a greater display of ensuring your prosperity.

For a considerable amount of the most widely recognized unending illnesses prodded by inflammation, the beginning stage is being overweight. What's more, being overweight is regularly the consequence of indulging foods that encourage inflammation. Most—however not all—of the foods that causes inflammation carry little sustenance.

Processed foods made with refined white flour and white sugar are top causes. These incorporate bundled white breads and rolls, microwavable products and treats. Soft drinks and other sugar-improved beverages are classified similarly.

Fats, for example, margarine, shortening and fat— additionally advance inflammation. So, do processed red meats, similar to bacon, hotdogs, sausage, salami and other store meats. Indeed, even lean red meat ought to be restricted to no more than one occasion per week.

Inflammation

Inflammation is a characteristic process with the natural cause to start healing by expanding dissemination. It is a mind-boggling procedure including both the safe framework and vascular framework and the transaction of different substances. Expanded blood flow brings white platelets and nutrients to the site of damage or contamination with the goal that attacking pathogens are killed and harm might be fixed. Trademark indications of inflammation include uneasiness (dolor), heat (calor), swelling (tumor) and redness (rubor).

In wider terms, inflammation is the body's safe framework's reaction to a stimulus. This can be because of normal wounds, for example, cutting your finger, or tumbling off of a bike, after which you feel the influenced zone become red, warm, and puffy – this is a confined reaction to damage, described by "expanded blood stream, hair-like enlargement, leucocyte invasion, and generation of synthetic mediators." In short, an inflammatory reaction implies that the natural (vague) safe framework is "battling against something that may end up being unsafe."

Notably, while inflammation is frequently seen in a negative light, it's really simple in limited quantities for insusceptible observation and host defense. In apparent "Goldilocks" structure, excessively small or a lot of inflammation both pose issues; truth be told, most unending illnesses are believed to be established in second rate inflammation that perseveres after some time. This inflammation may go unnoticed by the host (you!) until clear pathologies emerge, which include, however are not restricted to, diabetes, cardiovascular sickness, Nonalcoholic steatohepatitis , weight gain, immune system problems, Chron's disease, and even death. This idea is called "The inflammation hypothesis of ailment," in which inflammation is the regular hidden factor among the main sources of death.

There are atoms in the body called prostaglandins which assume a significant job in inflammation. It has been discovered that of the three fundamental kinds of prostaglandins, two of them (PG-E1 and PG-E3) have a modifying effect, while the third type (PG-E2) really advances inflammation. At the point when there is a lopsidedness in the body between these prostaglandins, inflammation can result. Prostaglandins are made in the body from fundamental unsaturated fats. You can help your body in making anti-inflammatory prostaglandins by eating vegetables, nuts, grains andseeds, for example, sesame and sunflower seeds. Then again, foods that cause a spike in insulin levels, for example, sugary nourishments, or nourishments with a high Glycemic burden advance generation of PG-E2 and increment inflammation.

An ordinary mitigating diet center around battling inflammation through the consumption of foods that lower insulin levels. To effectively lessen inflammation, you ought to in this manner eat foods that have a low Glycemic load, for example, entire grains, vegetables and lentils, and expend sound fats, for example, nuts, seeds, fish, additional virgin olive oil and fish. Flavors, for example, turmeric, ginger, and hot peppers additionally decrease inflammation. Simultaneously, you likewise need to reduce consumption of foods that are genius incendiary, for example, red meat, egg yolks and shellfish. Sugar is a key offender in inflammation, and in this way, you should likewise curtail sugary foods. Inflammation can likewise be decreased by taking enhancements, for example, fish oils which are high in Omega 3 unsaturated fats.

At the point when Inflammation Goes Awry:

While some inflammation is valuable and fitting for recuperating, endless or intemperate inflammation, filling no need produces harm. Interminable inflammation has a terrible notoriety since it is involved in different ailment procedures including (however not restricted to):

- Autoimmune sicknesses
- Joint pain

- Diabetes
- Alzheimer's sickness
- Atherosclerosis (solidifying of supply routes that prompts heart assault and stroke)
- ADD and ADHD
- Hypersensitivities and asthma
- Cancers
- Crohn's disease

Delicate tissue swelling and substance middle people engaged with inflammation can likewise disturb nerve endings, adding to pain.

What makes up an anti-inflammatory diet?

Prolonged second-rate inflammation is related to extreme oxidative pressure and changed glucose and lipid digestion in our (fat) cells, muscle, and liver. Therefore, investigation recommends that specific dietary changes can nip these key incendiary pathways and clinical pathologies. It is clarified that anti- inflammatory diet is the comprehension of how individual supplements influence the equivalent atomic targets influenced by pharmacological medications.

Convincing research from enormous scale, longitudinal observational examinations including the Women's Health Initiative Observational Study and Multi- Ethnic Study of Atherosclerosis (MESA) study, suggests that a diet with fitting calories that is low in refined starches, high in dissolvable fiber, high in mono unsaturated fats, a higher omega-3 to omega-6 proportion, and high in polyphenols, all have anti-inflammatory effects on the body. A Mediterranean diet design that combines olive oil, fish, modest lean meat consumption, and rich products of the soil, vegetables, and whole grains, indicates increasingly mitigating impacts when contrasted with an ordinary American diet. Other observational and interventional studies have additionally proposed that dietary examples joining green and dark tea, pecans, ground flaxseed, and garlic are likewise connected with decreased inflammation.

Correspondence between the fundamental insusceptible mechanism and the focal sensory system (CNS) is a basic, however, regularly neglected segment of the inflammatory reaction to tissue damage, illness or infection."

Social investigations have demonstrated that delayed mental pressure can actuate a similar genius inflammatory pathway we've been discussing earlier. While unending mental pressure can advance over-articulation of expert inflammatory arbiters, it can likewise advance indulging unhealthy foods without craving. Repetitively stress-eating calorie-rich, poorly nourishing foods not just further worsens mental pain and makes an endless loop of pressure eating, however, after some time advances adiposity, which we've portrayed is itself a genius inflammatory state.

In all honesty, inflammation begins as something to be thankful for. It happens when your body's defenses create white platelets and "warrior" mixes like eicosanoids to assault attacking infections, microorganisms, or poisons. An exemplary case of absolutely ordinary inflammation: pain, warmth, redness, and swelling around an injury or damage (think about a delicate sprained lower leg).

There's a different reaction called 'goals' that takes the pooches of war back to their sleeping quarters and recuperates your tissues. "The main period of inflammation causes cell decimation, and the subsequent stage, goals, starts cell revival. For whatever length of time that those stages are adjusted, you remain well."

However, for most of us, the parity never occurs. That is on the grounds that sugar, refined grains, and saturated fat can likewise trigger an inflammatory immune reaction, and the commonplace Western diet is filled with them, which means we're inflaming our bodies again and again, every time we eat. In the meantime, think about what the normal

American gets excessively little of: leafy foods, dull veggies – which are stuffed with cell reinforcements that help cooling and reduce the force of the underlying inflammatory reaction – and greasy fish, an incredible wellspring of omega-3 unsaturated fats, which can help move your body into the goals stage.

Air contamination and natural poisons likewise trigger your inflammatory immune responses along these lines, yet "the greater part of the ceaseless, additional inflammation in our bodies is diet-related. Endless inflammation can prompt coronary illness. In the mind, it's connected to tension and gloom. In your joints, it causes swelling and pain. In the gut, inflammation loses the equalization of supportive microscopic organisms and makes direct harm the walls of the digestion tracts.

Inflammation and Diet

You most likely have known about anti-inflammatory drugs. In any case, did you realize that there is a relationship that exists among inflammation and diet? Undoubtedly, there is such an unbelievably amazing anti-inflammatory diet which comprises of foods that counteract the beginning of inflammation.

Inflammation is essentially a restricted response of the cells and tissues in light of worrying contamination or damage. It is portrayed by pain, reddening and swelling, with genuine conditions joined by loss of development or even exertion. Basic inflammation conditions we know, incorporate joint inflammation and gout, however constant maladies, for example, coronary illness and stroke, can likewise be ascribed to some type of inflammation.

Ongoing research today connects inflammation to a wide scope of ceaseless ailments. Heart disease, depression, diabetes, and rheumatic fever appear to be altogether different as far as side effects; however, they are all similar due to one factor: inflammation. So, as to maintain a strategic distance from endless infections connected to inflammation, it is then critical to counteract and lessen the harm that this foundational inflammation can cause. What's more, indeed, you are correct - this should be possible through a solid, adjusted, mitigating diet.

The meals we eat can influence inflammation in an unusually intricate way. The best counsel to pursue is to keep away from "star incendiary foods" or foods that increase inflammation and take in a greater amount of mitigating food sources. This implies taking less of saturated fats found in meats, eggs, and dairy items which are rich in inflammation advancing arachidonic acid, while taking more or low-fat milk, lean meat, fish and vegetables. It is additionally essential to abstain from taking in an excessive amount of sugar as it isn't just identified with inflammation however to being overweight and numerous other unending ailments also.

The advantages of keeping up a sound diet free of processes doesn't not only liberate you from the danger of creating inflammation and conditions that go with it, it additionally gives long term benefits. You will in the end acknowledge how a decent anti-inflammatory diet can make your skin look more youthful, expel the hypersensitivity side effects, make your joints feel much improved, and give you a general solid inclination.

Omega-3 unsaturated fats in fish oil are one of the most significant viewpoints in a sound, anti-inflammatory diet. These basic unsaturated fats are extremely intense anti-inflammatory specialists that can shield and ease you from all types of inflammation. You can get your day by day portion of omega 3 fish oils through intake of satisfactory measures of fish and fish oils or take an ordinary portion of fish oil supplements. Make a point to counsel with your nutritionist or specialist in regard to suitable dose.

Beside the solid connection among inflammation and diet, look into concentrates additionally propose the significance of driving sound way of life propensities, for example, practicing normally, keeping up a perfect weight, limiting pressure, and evasion of smoking and liquor.

Chronic Inflammation and Diet

Late examinations have demonstrated that ceaseless inflammation could to a limited extent be in charge of the advancement of ailments like malignant growth, Alzheimer's infection, and rheumatoid joint inflammation.

What causes unending inflammation? Grouped factors evidently are at fault. For instance, poisons, stress, latency, less than stellar diet, and hereditary qualities are a portion of the presumed offenders.

In what capacity can endless inflammation be tended to? Here are some dietary approaches to lessen the hazard.

Food decisions. What we put in our bodies assumes a noteworthy job in our prosperity. Individuals who routinely devour inexpensive food, processed meats, greasy tidbits, and oily suppers don't charge so well on the wellbeing scale than people who eat all the more carefully. Actually, these individuals are leaving themselves open to an expanded danger of corpulence, elevated cholesterol, diabetes, and other undesirable conditions. To put it plainly, sustenance matters! Which choices will in general be ideal? Matured soy, green vegetables, grouped mushrooms, new natural products, extra-virgin olive oil, cold-water fish, green and dark tea, nuts, and red wine (with some restraint) are great decisions. Simultaneously, it is likewise imperative to purchase natural at whatever point achievable. As we probably are aware, natural yields are those that have not been splashed with pesticides.

Vitamins and supplements. Normally, the ideal path for getting basic vitamins, minerals, and supplements in the body is by eating whole foods: crisp vegetables and natural products are particularly great decisions. In any case, customary access to crisp food isn't constantly feasible for certain individuals. Along these lines, fantastic enhancements might be required. Which types are best in battling inflammation? Ones that contain vitamins C, D, and E, folic acid, selenium, carotenoids, fish oil, coQ10, tumeric or cucumin, garlic, and ginger. NOTE: Always check with your PCP before taking enhancements: particular types may meddle with prescription or intensify the impacts of specific medications (like blood thinners).

Fiber. Fiber merits a class all its own on the grounds that its advantages are stunning. Standard intake of this miracle has been thought to reduce conditions like coronary illness, elevated cholesterol, and certain malignancies. Which type of fiber is best in battling inflammation? The dissolvable assortment like those found in beans, oat grain, lentils, apples, nuts, seeds, and strawberries. Insoluble types like those found in whole grains and wheat grain additionally fill a need since they will in general get things going along in our stomach related tract. Taking in the middle of 25 to 35 grams of fiber for every day, with roughly 2/3 originating from the dissolvable grouping, is believed to be certain. Strikingly, while different starches, similar to white flour and sugar, ought to be disregarded however much as could be expected, solvent fiber carbs are unquestionably not miscreants.

There are different approaches to limit inflammation notwithstanding nourishment. Exercise, yoga, and hurling the cigarettes (and when you smoke) strengthen an anti-inflammatory diet.

Some Insight on How an Anti-Inflammatory Diet Works

There is anything but a formal diet plan that frameworks precisely what to eat, its amount, and when. Or maybe, the mitigating diet is tied in with filling your suppers with nourishment that have been appeared to battle inflammation and — similarly as significant — removing foods that have been appeared to add to it.

Think about the mitigating diet as a way of life as opposed to an diet. "An anti-inflammatory diet is an eating plan that attempts to reduce or limit poor quality inflammation inside our bodies,"

In a perfect world, you would eat seven to nine servings of leafy foods every day, limit your intake of red meat and dairy, pick complex sugars over straightforward ones, and swear off processed sustenance.

You'll need to pick foods that are rich in omega-3 unsaturated fats — including anchovies, salmon, halibut, and mussels — as opposed to omega-6 unsaturated fats, which are found in corn oil, vegetable oil, mayonnaise, plate of mixed greens dressings, and many processed meals.

Eating along these lines is a smart thought for everybody on the grounds that huge numbers of the foods with the possibility to prompt inflammation aren't sound at any rate. Everybody can profit by constraining or disposing of sugar and exceptionally processed foods and choosing unsaturated fats, organic products, vegetables, nuts, seeds, and slender proteins.

The Anti-inflammatory diet could be particularly useful for somebody who's managing interminable inflammation because of a wellbeing condition. Competitors and individuals who exercise at a high rate and are hoping to decrease their standard inflammation could likewise think that it's valuable.

Step by step instructions to recognize Anti-inflammatory diet

In any case, the arrangement with the most research- sponsored anti-inflammatory cred is the customary Mediterranean diet, underscoring natural products, vegetables, whole grains, vegetables, fish, and olive oil. A few extremely enormous investigations—including the renowned Nurses' Health Study—have discovered that individuals who pursue a Mediterranean example of eating have lower levels of the incendiary markers C- responsive protein and interleukin-6 in their blood contrasted and the individuals who don't. This might be one cause the Mediterranean diet is connected to such a large number of medical advantages, from holding weight down to cutting heart and stroke chance.

The objectives of an AI plan are basic: Cut route back on foods that trigger an incendiary reaction and eat a greater amount of the foods that mend harm. While there are a few varieties in what's permitted and what isn't, most AI plans share an accentuation on eating whole, insignificantly processed foods, bright vegetables, monounsaturated fats like olive oil and avocado, beautiful berries and other organic product, and loads of omega-3s from greasy fish (or enhancements), and staying away from included sugar and refined grains.

All things considered, your plate may appear to be somewhat unique from your companion's or coworker's, and that is the manner in which it ought to be. Meals sensitivities assume a job, as well: People respond to foods in an unexpected way, and in the event that somebody has an affectability to a specific nourishment, it will prompt cytokine creation and an increase in other incendiary synthetic concoctions.

What the Research Says

There's a lot of research demonstrating the negative impacts of inflammation. It's related with medical problems from diabetes and Alzheimer's to disease and weight.

A few different investigations have taken a gander at the impact eating an diet rich in anti-inflammatory foods can have on certain wellbeing conditions. For example, choosing anti-inflammatory foods may help individuals with rheumatoid joint pain (RA). Following an diet like this won't really fix you, yet it might help decrease the disease's effect, defer movement, reduce how much drug is required, and lessen joint harm.

Different investigations have discovered anti- inflammatory foods can:

- Help competitors recuperate
- Manage pain related with aging

- Protect the heart
- Improve personal satisfaction for individuals with numerous sclerosis

A Food List of What to Eat on an Anti- Inflammatory Diet

Following anti-inflammatory diet means stacking up on foods that examination has indicated can help lower inflammation, and reducing your intake of meals that have the contrary impact. Probably the best thing about the diet is there are a lot of sustenance alternatives and a lot of squirm room so you can pick and pick the foods you like best.

In the event that you need somewhat more structure, consider embracing the Mediterranean diet. There's a great deal of cover with the anti-inflammatory diet in light of the fact that both underscores eating organic products, vegetables, and whole grains.

Foods to Eat

- Fresh organic product, including grapefruit, grapes, blueberries, bananas, apples, mangos, peaches, tomatoes, and pomegranates
- Dried organic product, including plums

- Vegetables, particularly broccoli, Brussels sprouts, cauliflower, and bok choy
- Plant-based proteins, for example, chickpeas, seitan, and lentils
- Fatty fish, for example, salmon, sardines, tuna fish, herring, lake trout, and mackerel
- Whole grains, including oats, dark colored rice, grain, and whole wheat bread
- Leafy greens, including kale, spinach, and romaine lettuce
- Ginger
- Nuts, including pecans and almonds
- Seeds, for example, chia seeds and flaxseed
- Foods loaded up with omega-3 unsaturated fats, for example, avocado and olive oil
- Coffee
- Green tea
- Dark chocolate (with some restraint)
- Red wine (with some restraint)

What conditions can a mitigating diet help?

Specialists, dietitians, and naturopaths prescribe anti- inflammatory eats less carbs as an integral treatment for some conditions that are intensified by unending inflammation.

A mitigating diet can support numerous conditions, including:

- Rheumatoid joint pain
- Psoriasis
- Asthma
- Eosinophilic esophagitis
- Crohn's sickness
- Colitis
- Inflammatory inside illness
- Diabetes
- Obesity
- Metabolic disorder
- Heart sickness
- Lupus
- Hashimoto's sickness

Also, eating a mitigating diet can help reduce the danger of specific malignant growths, including colorectal disease.

What Are the Possible Health Benefits of Following an Anti-Inflammatory Diet?

Following an anti-inflammatory diet has been appeared to help individuals with:

- Autoimmune issue
- Heart disease
- Cancer, including bosom malignancy and colorectal disease
- Alzheimer's disease
- Diabetes
- Pulmonary disease
- Epilepsy

CHAPTER TWO

The Benefits Of Anti-Inflammatory Foods

Lately, inflammation has turned into a blasting point at the front line of wellbeing and health. It is one of the main sources of maturing and disease, nonetheless, much of the time, it is preventable. Our cutting-edge ways of life where we progressively experience the ill effects of interminable pressure, rest less hours than our bodies need and eat consumes less calories poor in anti-inflammation supplements, have prompted constant inflammation in the body.

On a positive note, so as to counteract ceaseless inflammation in the body, we can pursue an anti- inflammatory diet that helps keep the resistant mechanisms solid, balances weight and keeps all the body's mechanism working ideally.

What does the anti-inflammatory diet comprise of?

This diet centers around wiping out the nourishments that cause inflammatory reactions in the body, similar to gluten, dairy, sugar and processed foods, and trading them for wholefoods, for example, vegetables, vegetables, whole grains, fish and natural product.

The foods most extravagant in anti-inflammatory vitamins you ought to incorporate into your diet are:

- Green vegetables, for example, spinach and kale
- Celery
- Coconut oil
- Turmeric
- Ginger
- Chia Seeds
- Beetroot
- Broccoli
- Blueberries
- Salmon
- Walnuts

As should be obvious, they are meals that are anything but difficult to consolidate into your diet every day. They will counteract untimely maturing and ailments, improve subjective capacity, reinforce the resistant mechanisms and lift vitality levels. Lift your wellbeing and essentialness with the anti-inflammatory diet!

In contrast to the ordinary diet, it doesn't have a snappy name. Nor does it guarantee you'll drop a size by Saturday. It's not even extremely an diet, in essence, however really an eating plan forever. It's the alleged anti-inflammatory diet - or rather, anti-inflammatory slims down. About at least six diet books depend on the anti-inflammatory thought - and various Web destinations advance "mitigating" eating.

The anti-inflammatory diet is perfect for by and large great wellbeing. Defenders of the diet state it can lessen coronary illness hazard, hold existing heart issues under tight restraints, reduce blood triglycerides and circulatory strain, and calm delicate and hardened ligament joints. In any case, specialists yield that enemy of inflammation eating is more compelling for some medical issues than others – and that the logical proof for the disease decrease advantages of these eating plans is as yet being assembled.

Anti-inflammatory Diets: What Do You Eat?

Particulars differ from diet to slim down, yet when all is said in done mitigating diets recommend:

- Eat a lot of foods grown from the ground.

- Minimize immersed and trans fats.

- Eat a decent wellspring of omega-3 unsaturated fats, for example, fish or fish oil enhancements and pecans.

- Watch your intake of refined starches, for example, pasta and white rice.

- Eat a lot of whole grains, for example, dark colored rice and bulgur wheat.

- Eat lean protein sources, for example, chicken; cut back on red meat and full-fat dairy meals.

- Avoid refined nourishments and processed foods.

- Spice it up. Ginger, curry, and different flavors can have an anti-inflammatory impact.

As one case of multi-day of anti-inflammatory eating, a morning meal of toasted steel-cut oats with berries, yogurt, or other fixing and espresso or green tea. Lunch could be fish serving of mixed greens on 7-grain bread and a smoothie with occasional natural products. For a tidbit, attempt an ounce of dark chocolate and around four pecans. Supper could be spaghetti with turkey meat sauce, spinach serving of mixed greens with oranges and pecans, and apple cranberry pie made without spread.

The diets don't guarantee weight reduction, yet weight decrease does frequently happen. What's more, that bodes well, given the cosmetics of the diet, says Greenfield.

"When you are looking at curtailing red meat, dairy, fats and trans fats, halfway hydrogenated oils, profoundly processed carbs - and eating more beneficial protein like fish, eating more products of the soil - chances are that individuals will lose in any event a smidgen of weight."

Nourishment High in Omega-6: Omega-3 proportion

With an end goal to decrease inflammation, it is suggested that you stay away from foods that have a high proportion of Omega-6 to Omega-3. Coming up next is a rundown of some basic foods that will in general have a high proportion.

1. Grains - 20:1
2. Seed and seed oils - 70:1
3. Soybean oil - 7:1
4. Chicken - 15:1
5. Potato Chips - 60:1

Advantages of Omega-3

The long-chain types of Omega-3 greasy acids are DHA and EPA. DHA is the structure square of cerebrum tissue and EPA is its forerunner. Here are a list of the advantages and conditions that are improved with Omega-3 acids in the diet.

1. Healthier, more grounded bones
2. Improved state of mind guideline
3. Reduced danger of Parkinson's
4. Reduced danger of death from ALL causes
5. Prevention of vascular difficulties from Type-II diabetes
6. Gallstones
7. Multiple Sclerosis
8. Brain and eye improvement in children
9. Peripheral corridor sickness
10. Preventing post birth anxiety
11. Combating malignant growth

Foods High in Omega-3

1. Flax seed oil
2. Canola Oil
3. Walnuts
4. Fish
5. Shellfish
6. Krill
7. Cod liver oil
8. Omega-3 enhanced eggs
9. Pasture-raised meats
10. Wild rice
11. Beans

Anti-inflammatory Foods

Alongside concentrating on foods that will give the right proportion of Omega-6 to Omega-3 unsaturated fats, there are likewise sure foods that have mitigating properties:

1. Vegetables

2. Fruit

3. Sweet potatoes and different tubers

4. Dark Chocolate

5. Red wine

6. Coffee and tea

7. Ginger, turmeric, garlic and different flavors

8. Olive oil, Coconut oil and spread

A quality fish oil supplement should be in your diet. It's imperative to search for fish oil that has been molecularly refined and contains in any event 500mg of both DHA and EPA. There are a lot of fish oil supplements available that will promote 1000mg of fish oil, yet not all contain the suggested measure of those two acids.

The anti-inflammatory diet isn't generally an diet; it's a greater amount of an eating plan. Furthermore, and when you do a little inquiry about it, you'll see that there's not only one anti-inflammatory diet; there are a few, each with an alternate turn. For our motivations here, I've attempted to show what a "nonexclusive" adaptation is. This form shares with the others the idea that proceeded and wild inflammation prompts ailment and that following an eating plan that abstains from aggravating the body advances wellbeing and can help forestall ailment.

As a rule, a mitigating diet incorporates:

- Plenty of foods grown from the ground
- Plenty of whole grains (e.g., darker rice, bulgur wheat)
- Lean protein (e.g., chicken, fish)
- Anti-inflammatory flavors (e.g., curry, ginger)
- Omega-3 unsaturated fats, (for example, those found in fish, fish oil enhancements, and pecans)
- A decrease in
- Refined starches (e.g., pasta, white rice)
- Red meat and full-fat dairy foods
- Saturated and trans fats
- No refined or processed foods

A note in regards to this arrangement: The impacts you experience (i.e., an improvement in your indications) won't be as quick as they would be in the event that you treated yourself with prescriptions. You most likely need to give the anti-inflammatory diet in any event two weeks versus the hour or two a prescription may take. On the other hand, this diet may have a reward impact not generally found in prescriptions: weight reduction!

The Easiest Changes to Boost Health - Anti- Inflammatory Diet

There are a million and one stylish diets out there offering to change what you look like and feel in merely days. The purchaser is overflowed with items that will cause their skin "to show up" more advantageous and milder to contact. In a world with an excess of spotlight on looking great and "showing up" more advantageous, there is one diet that WILL make you more beneficial and possibly carry on with a more drawn out life in your enemy of matured body.

The anti-inflammatory diet has such a large number of employments today it is astounding all of the wellbeing, wellness and experts have not hopped on the most straightforward of diet changes and promoted them as the following huge pattern in weight reduction, excellence and anti-aging. The truth of the matter is the anti-inflammatory diet can do everything different diets guarantee they can do and build life expectancy all the while.

The Benefits of Natural Anti Inflammatory These Days

Regular enemy of inflammatories are prudent, and individuals are currently much better instructed in what is great and terrible for them. Clearly setting off to the burger bar every day, or eating gigantic amounts of nourishment superfluously is awful for you, and ought to be kept away from. Probably the most straightforward approaches to ease pain brought about by inflammation is to pursue a diet dependent on characteristic enemy of inflammatories. This implies eating more products of the soil, fish, and chicken, while eliminating bread, intemperate sugar, starches, and processed or bundled nourishment.

Omega-3 unsaturated fats repress the action of the catalysts that crush the ligament tissues in the joints. They normally decrease inflammation and lessen pain. Fish is one of the better wellsprings of Omega-3, and ought to be eaten consistently. A standard measurement of Omega-3 as unadulterated fish oil enhancements is awesome for good joints.

What we should take a gander at are regular cures given by such things as turmeric, ginger, rosemary, and green tea. These are for the most part characteristic enemy of inflammatories items which will decrease swelling in joints. Dark green vegetable, avocados, and pecans can be eaten consistently, and healthful oils, for example, evening primrose can be accepted day by day as enhancement.

Just as what we ought to eat, there is an whole host of foods we ought to stay away from. We should constrain our intake of red meat, dairy items, and immersed fats. We should cook foods with olive oil rather than vegetable oil and cut down on animal proteins. Eating a lot of fiber that are found in leafy foods regular is additionally prescribed, as is drinking tea as opposed to espresso. It is additionally prudent to drink up to eight glasses of water multi day.

Adjacent to that, an diet dependent on the common enemy of inflammatories is presently generally utilized and accepted to have the option to help you keeping your wellbeing stay ideal and furthermore influence the recuperating procedure of individuals who have endless inflammation issues

Common Anti-Inflammatory Foods for Better Health And Less Pain

Inflammation is perceived by pain, swelling, redness and warmth around the influenced territory. There are various choices to treat inflammation. One is prescriptions, which so far hasn't been best since it doesn't generally fix the issue. The other choice is the normal way, from where our body begins from; our body been made ordinarily and gets its regular items from nature. This implies choosing the nourishment that your body needs, since deficiencies of certain fixings no doubt caused the sickness in any case. It is likewise known that our body can respond distinctively to foods, since certain foods being utilized diverse to other people. What that implies is that inflammation a few foods can have a positive or a negative outcome. Here are a portion of the regular anti-inflammatory foods; whenever chosen effectively, they will have that effect in recuperating.

Normal Anti-Inflammatory Foods

Vegetables and organic products: Vegetables and products of green and splendid shading help the procedure of inflammatory conditions. Vegetables and organic products are rich in cell reinforcements, for example, vitamins, minerals, fiber which the body needs each day to remain sound. There are numerous assortments, per model, squash, sweet potatoes, avocados, beans, lentils, dark green vegetables and cruciferous vegetables. These have numerous cancer prevention agents, phytochemicals, and mitigating properties present.

Significant Fats

Likewise, rich in anti-inflammatory foods are olive oil, coconut oil, salmon, sardines, and avocados. Every one of them contain omega 3 unsaturated fats which are fundamental for inflammation and joint wellbeing. The acid from omega 3 is a provocative operator that changes into prostaglandins which is a hormone like substance. Omega 3 isn't valuable for joint pain and inflammation, it is additionally significant for wellbeing all in all. We just can get omega from our diet, hence it is essential to incorporate a portion of the solid oils such olive, coconut, macadamia and krill, which is more grounded than fish oil. There are numerous choices of foods accessible which contain an assortment of omega.

Oils you should think about

Olive oil has more medical advantages not many people know of. Make a point to utilize it in your diet however much as could be expected. Olive oil is high in cancer prevention agents and is containing a substance called oleuropein. Medicinal science has verified that additional virgin olive oil is perhaps the most advantageous food we can add to our diet. This oil is most useful and viable for joint inflammation sufferers since it can cool inflammation and simplicity joint pain. Be that as it may, for cooking, searing, heating and so on utilize just coconut or macadamia nut oil. Different oils when warmed become lethal and more often than not transform into trans fats which can trigger inflammation and joint pain, just as other medical problems. Maintain a strategic distance from these oils: Vegetable oils, soybean, canola, these are the more typical ones the vast majority think about in light of the names. Truly, they have a solid sounding name, yet they are not beneficial.

Flavors

Turmeric would be over the rundown in lessening inflammation and joint pain. Also, turmeric has a compound curcumin which is known for some, medical advantages and has the ability to fix joint pain. It is best utilized in its characteristic fine structure and added to your diet when possible, the more the better. Other significant flavors utilized for reducing inflammation are cinnamon, rosemary, garlic, ginger and oregano. These are high in polyphenols and bioflavonoids which help to reduce inflammation just as ward off free radicals. Cayenne pepper is additionally known for its mitigating property and its capsicum content which is added to certain creams for help with discomfort.

Grains

Whole grains which contain starches can likewise help in averting spikes in the sugar level of the blood, as it is realized that sugar advances inflammation. In any case, utilize just non refined whole grains, when preparing has occurred all the integrity is lost, for example, vitamins, minerals and fiber. Among the best grains are oats: Whole oats, whole wheat, quinoa, couscous and Bulgar. To take a multi-supplement is of advantage, it can fill the spot of certain food you generally may not get from your diet as required every day. In any case, your first need should consistently be the diet, just than when taking an enhancement, you will get best esteem.

Eating Anti Inflammatory Herbs and Diets

I've been doing a great deal of research as of late into inflammation and how it influences our ways of life and nature of living. Eating anti-inflammatory diet and herbs is by all accounts a larger method for expanding the nature of an individual's life over a significant lot of ime. In the present day and age, individuals are living longer than at any other time. Yet, is the nature of that life improving also? One needs to ask themselves the inquiry, it extremely beneficial to live till I'm 90 if the most recent 15 years of my life are loaded up with things as Alzheimer chemotherapy, and joint pain? It appears that despite the fact that individuals are living longer and more, the measure of sicknesses and afflictions present in the cutting-edge world appear to be on the ascent too.

A major cause for this is by all accounts the diets that we eat. It isn't figured anybody would contend that the standard diet is loaded up with foods that aren't generally such solid. The sheer volume of additives, fake hues and sugars, pesticides, processed foods, and different things in the diet is really amazing. A great part of the diet appears to realize a general condition of inflammation inside the body. Inflammation as an idea is an awesome thing, shielding areas of our bodies from unsafe and perilous things. Inflammation happens when an individual gets bit by a noxious bug, or when an abrupt effect causes gruff power injury to a specific locale of the body. By swelling and separating the district, the body can best shield itself from further mischief and find a way to fix the harm.

An issue appears to happen when the body is empowers toward an expert provocative state through the consumption of specific foods. Diets by and large are said to either be inflammatory or star provocative. As you can envision, foods that are master incendiary will expand the measure of inflammation an individual encounters in different parts of their body. Pain will for the most part increment, and the danger of numerous endless illnesses likewise appears to go up. Sustenance like low quality foods, quick foods, sugar, processed sustenance and high fat meats are at the highest priority on the rundown of anti-inflammatory foods. As an individual's body goes into a raised condition of inflammation, comparing diseases like joint inflammation appear to develop progressively extraordinary and increasingly agonizing too.

Expending foods that for the most part advance an anti- inflammatory state appears to positively affect an individual's wellbeing and health as time goes on. There is a great deal of writing that has just been expounded on anti-inflammatory diets and anybody inspired by the theme should keep on doing research regarding the matter. I at first began inquiring about the theme when made mindful that joint pain keeps running in my family. I needed to check whether there was whatever I could do that would help stop the joint pain before it at any point began. That carried me to inquiring about anti-inflammatory foods and herbs. I found that all in all, to keep an attitude of staying away from foods that caused Inflammation in the body would prompt a general condition of health and would enable the body to battle interminable ailments like joint pain and different things. So, as it were, having a legacy of joint inflammation in my family was right around a gift since it drove me to look into about approaches to improve my general wellbeing. anti- inflammatory herbs and diets are certainly something that merit thought.

How Inflammation Triggers Diabetes - And Anti-Inflammatory Tips to Live By

Inflammation is rising as a key factor hidden the advancement of type 2 diabetes, and it's one that numerous individuals have not known about. A typical and totally common body reaction, inflammation is a procedure by which your white platelets and body synthetic substances shield you from microorganisms, infections and disease.

You can identify intense inflammation in your body by redness, warmth, swelling and pain at the site of damage. These are signs that your body is effectively battling a contamination.

In any case, under numerous conditions - regularly because of way of life factors or an over-responsive resistant mechanism - inflammation can end up endless, prompting a poor-quality condition of decay in your body. For this situation, inflammation causes no apparent indications despite the fact that it might make harm your mechanism, which is the cause it's otherwise called "quiet" inflammation.

Constant "quiet" inflammation isn't just embroiled in ceaseless infections like coronary illness, malignancy, Alzheimer's disease and rheumatoid joint inflammation, yet additionally in type 2 diabetes.

Your Diet and Your Lifestyle Habits Can Increase Inflammation Too

Numerous variables can invigorate incessant inflammation in your body, including:

1. Overweight and corpulence
2. Unhealthy diet
3. Poorly controlled diabetes
4. Lack of activity
5. Gum sickness
6. Smoking
7. Stress
8. Long-term contaminations

You will see that numerous things on this rundown - unhealthy diet, absence of activity, gum ailment - additionally increment your type 2 diabetes hazard, so and when you need to stay away from diabetes, it's critical to find a way to decrease the inflammation in your body.

This incorporates:

- Avoiding expert inflammatory foods. The following foods may add to foundational inflammation: trans fats (found in mostly hydrogenated vegetable oil), singed sustenance, sugar, bread and other refined carbs, soft drink, liquor, and polyunsaturated vegetable oils.

- Eating a lot of anti-inflammatory foods. Foods that help reduce inflammation incorporate crisp products of the soil, and wild-got fish (for the omega-3 fats).

- Exercising

- Quitting smoking

- Reducing worry in your life

- Considering certain anti-inflammatory herbs and flavors, for example, turmeric, ginger and boswellia.

It's critical to downplay constant inflammation in your body to decrease your danger of type 2 diabetes as well as various other endless sicknesses.

How would you know whether you have chronic inflammation?

The C-Reactive Protein (CRP) test is the most widely recognized test used to distinguish inflammation; it gauges a protein in your body that increments during fundamental inflammation. In one investigation, ladies with raised CRP levels were observed to be almost multiple times bound to create diabetes than those with lower levels - and even in the wake of modifying for other hazard factors, the hazard was still more than multiple times as high.

Nonetheless, regardless of whether you realize you have raised CRP levels or not, it's a smart thought to make the strides above to decrease inflammation in your body. We all are affected by inflammation to changing degrees, and the best alternative to keep the perpetual, diabetes-connected type away is to lead a sound way of life as depicted previously.

You may likewise consider fish oil supplements which can be extremely high in omega 3 unsaturated fats which have been appeared in research concentrates to go about as an anti-inflammation, accordingly reducing your danger of cardiovascular illness and different ailments. Omega 3 fish oil unsaturated fats, especially EPA, have a constructive outcome on your provocative reaction. By helping the body produce anti-inflammatory eicosanoids, Omega 3 unsaturated fats help your body control it's inflammation cycle, which avoids and alleviates difficult conditions and ailment. For grown-ups, fish oil supplements with omega 3 improve memory, review, thinking just as center and fixation.

Magnesium is a Powerful Natural Anti- Inflammatory Mineral

While magnesium has consistently been known to be an extremely incredible mineral, another investigation including 3,713 postmenopausal ladies has completely demonstrated its anti-inflammatory impacts. With 100 mg of magnesium for every day, anti-inflammatory properties were experienced. Magnesium could be of extraordinary guide to the individuals who wish to stay away from the awful reactions of anti-inflammatory pharmaceuticals.

As per the investigation, inflammatory markers, for example, CRP (C-responsive protein), TNFa (tumor rot factor alpha), and IL6 (interleukin 6) were altogether reduced when magnesium intake was expanded. This implies magnesium assumes an immediate job in bringing down basic provocative markers, further demonstrating its helpful properties.

Inflammation has been attached to endless ailments, making millions endure every day. Utilizing magnesium to help in the battle against inflammation is a savvy choice, and one that requires no pharmaceuticals.

Do You Know About the Fish Oil Anti- Inflammation Diet?

Have you at any point pondered, for what cause are media humming such a great amount on hostile to inflammation diet? This is a direct result of the stunning finishes of numerous examinations on hindering inflammation in the body. Hyper- inflammation can be the main driver of numerous wellbeing concerns, running from minor ones like - wrinkles, male pattern baldness, and sensitivities to significant ones like heart assaults, disease, joint pain, and psoriasis, and so on.

An enemy of inflammation diet will bode well in the event that we comprehend what sustenance sources have inflammation impact and what does not have? At that point it will be simple for us to choose the inflammation free diet that we as a whole have been longing for.

Nuts, tofu, flaxseeds, ocean bottom like fish, shrimps and clams are rich wellsprings of Omega 3 unsaturated fats, while chicken, hamburger, pork, different oils like sunflower oil, hemp oil, pumpkin oil, and so forth are rich in omega 6 unsaturated fats.

As you may have speculated; as a result of our dietary patterns (we eat a great deal of slick, seared and lousy nourishment), a large portion of us have elevated amounts of Omega 6 fats (they have inflammation property) and are insufficient in omega 3 fats. The perfect proportion of omega6 to omega3 for a sound body is 4:1 however much of the time, it is as high as 50:1. Along these lines, we need an enemy of inflammation diet (omega 3 fats) to counter impact the inflammation in the body.

Studies have demonstrated that DHA omega3 fat can be changed over to a compound substance called Resolvin D2. D2 is an awesome inflammation specialist. In this way sustenance sources that are rich in DHA ought to be incorporated into our everyday diet routine to control body's inflammation cycle.

Slick and cold-water fish, similar to wild salmon, hoki, halibut, mackerel, herring, and sardines are rich in DHA. In any case, due to the expanding contamination in the sea waters, fish in them will in general gather poisons as well. Consequently, eating them routinely isn't suggested.

A simple choice is to take fish oil supplements. These enhancements experience the different refining procedures to sift through all the destructive poisons and synthetic concoctions like mercury, lead, arsenic, PCBs, and so on. Accordingly, with their consumption you can achieve wanted degrees of DHA and EPA with no stresses of polluting influences.

In one of the clinical preliminaries, it was seen that enhancements produced using the blend of hoki oil and fish oil have more than double the anti-inflammatory impact as in contrast with different enhancements. Unadulterated and high DHA fish oil supplement, can go about as a powerful enemy of inflammation diet. It, other than decreasing the soreness in your body will likewise expand your future.

CHAPTER THREE

What Can I Do To Reduce Inflammation In My Body?

What Causes Inflammation in the Body and How to Control It?

Inflammation in the body is really useful and is treated as a major aspect of body's guard mechanism.

It goes about as a layer between the external condition and the influenced territory; it likewise represses the disease to spread to other body parts. If there should arise an occurrence of any damage or disease, we see redness and soreness around the influenced territory. This is on the grounds that; the WBCs (white platelets) are joined to the internal linings of veins around influenced territory.

Then again, if due to any cause, if WBCs begin regarding solid cells as remote material, increasingly more of WBCs begin gathering at the internal linings, bringing about pain and overabundance of soreness around there. This results in endless inflammation, which if not controlled at before stages can prompt difficult conditions like Arthritis, Psoriasis, and so on.

In the wake of understanding what causes inflammation, let us currently discover a successful method for controlling it.

The best and regular approach to have a tab on the body's inflammation cycle is to accomplish elevated amounts of DHA omega3 unsaturated fats. These are long chain polyunsaturated fats, which are required by the body for its legitimate development and improvement. Studies have demonstrated that the body can change over DHA to a synthetic called Resolvin D2 that has a property to respond with internal linings of veins to shape Nitric Oxide. This layer of Nitric oxides hinders abundance of WBCs to join the internal linings of veins, and thus help in reducing Inflammation.

In this manner, it is our enthusiasm to have high DHA levels. Be that as it may, since body can't deliver DHA all alone, we need to take express activities to incorporate high DHA sustenance sources in our everyday diet.

Cold-water fish like Hoki, Tuna, Salmon, and so on are the rich wellspring of DHA fats. In any case, in view of expanding water contamination, fish are additionally loaded with pollutions like mercury, lead, arsenic, and so forth. Clearly, it's anything but a decent arrangement to lessen inflammation in the body at the expense of eating poisons.

This is the place fish oil enhancements come to help. They experience refining procedures to expel all the undesirable and destructive synthetic compounds from the oil. Consequently, are useful for human consumption.

Since you realize what causes inflammation in the body and how you can control the equivalent, your subsequent stage ought to be invest some more energy in web, discover a viable enhancement and begin taking it right away.

Perpetual Inflammation in the Body is Dangerous

You know when you have a sore throat and your lymph hubs are swollen? Your body has sent in the military of white platelets to wreck the encompassing tissue and improve. The issue comes when it doesn't quit obliterating sound tissue and continues onward.

Specialists have connected inflammation in your body with illnesses of different types. Asthma, rheumatoid joint pain, coronary illness, considerably malignant growth and memory misfortune.

Studies demonstrate it's basic to your wellbeing and prosperity to control inflammation in the body.

You may consider inflammation swollen joints from joint pain or swelling encompassing a paper cut however inflammation can likewise be inside where it's not obvious.

Excited corridors cause plaque development and stop up the entry adding to a heart assault. Moreover, inflammation in your cerebrum stops up the neuron pathways so the messages aren't clear or don't get sent- - this can prompt Alzheimer's.

Inflammation begins as your body's barrier against damage or sickness. It's extremely your body's method for healing you. However, when its work is done, the inflammation should shop. Chronic inflammation can cause long term harm.

The Guide to Getting Rid Of Inflammation in Your Body

Huge numbers of us experience the ill effects of inflammation in our bodies. Nonetheless, so as to realize how to reduce inflammation in the body we should comprehend what inflammation truly is. Inflammation is a procedure brought about by our bodies, to shield us from unsafe diseases or infection. In the event that you experience the ill effects of inflammation in your body, you will have encountered redness or pain. In like manner, to explore there are numerous causes for inflammation. Inflammation can be intense or incessant, whichever way there are a few things that you can do to dispose of it. Along these lines, how about we begin examining how to lessen inflammation in the body.

Decreasing this issue in your body is certifiably not a troublesome assignment. So as to do this you should watch what you eat and practice normally. How about we talk about each in detail. When attempting to stay away from inflammation in your body; you should reduce your intake of processed foods. All and any type of handled foods will contain sustenance that builds the inflammation level in your body. Additionally, attempt to maintain a strategic distance from sustenance that contain high measures of sugar. Consequently, so as to anticipate the issue you should eat vegetables and organic products. Vegetables and natural products contain mitigating properties. These foods have demonstrated to reduce inflammation in the whole body. It is proposed to expend the vegetables and natural products that are brilliant in shading.

Additionally, in your customary eating diet increment the intake of omega-3 unsaturated fat. Omega-3 greasy is generally found in various kinds of nuts and seeds. Accordingly, make a propensity to eat pecans or sesame seeds all the time. Research demonstrates that green tea and straightforward water can likewise help keep this issue from happening. Green tea and water are referred to go about as cell reinforcements, accordingly with normal use they will limit the issue. Aside from watching what you eat, practicing has additionally demonstrated to help in keeping this from occurring. With exercise you will shed pounds, when you get in shape the measure of weight on your joints will be less. The less weight on your joints will likewise help forestall an inflammation issue. Nonetheless, you should guarantee that you normally practice for in any event 40 minutes.

The previously mentioned systems are best in assisting with inflammation in the body. In any case, you can likewise take supplements which are rich in fish oil or vitamins. Likewise, alongside these enhancements ordinary body back rubs have additionally demonstrated to help in preventing this from occurring. These back rubs should be possible with oil or basic creams. You can likewise keep warmed cushions on your body, which will absolutely help. Despite the fact that these methods work, they are not as compelling as the adjusting of the diet and working out. In this way, when attempting to ensure the body you ought to consistently select to initially control what you eat and practice normally. Keep in mind, that regardless of what procedure you pick you have to guarantee that you are steady with it. Inflammation is treatable just in the event that you are given.

Step by step instructions to Reduce Chronic Inflammation in Your Body

Joint inflammation, Bursitis, Tendonitis, Plantar Fasciitis, Colitis, Dermatitis, Pancreatitis, Appendicitis, Sinusitis - what do these conditions share practically speaking? Since they end with the addition that they are each of the indication of inflammation in your body. Once in a while inflammation is only a sign or abuse or mileage, yet in some cases something in the resistant mechanism has gone astray inciting far reaching and changed and some of the time exceptionally crippling incendiary issues. So how about we investigate the components that impact inflammation and either lose or keep the resistant mechanism on track.

1. Food sensitivities – in the rundown event that somebody is giving indications of an incendiary condition is to survey and expel nourishment hypersensitivities from their diet. Nearly everybody has sustenance sensitivities - in testing more than 500 patients everything except 3 have had nourishment hypersensitivities. The vast majority have no clue they do on the grounds that the indications of some sustenance sensitivities can be postponed and inconspicuous, few out of every odd nourishment hypersensitivity is as emotional or dangerous as a nut sensitivity. Sensitivities that are interceded by antibodies can cause such wide and changed

manifestations as clogging, loose bowels, swelling, gas, sinus blockage, joint pain, cerebral pains, exhaustion, skin rashes, dermatitis, psoriasis, skin inflammation, sniffling, runny nose, watery eyes, and irritated mouth/nose/ears. Eating something you are adversely affected by strains your invulnerable mechanism and incites inordinate inflammation.

2. The stomach related tract - abundance of unfortunate microscopic organisms or yeast in the stomach related tract can make a harmed/aroused stomach related tract. This thus implies the invulnerable mechanism isn't working appropriately since 70-80% of your insusceptible mechanism is situated around your stomach related tract. This unfortunate condition and possible absence of good microorganisms, alluded to as probiotic microscopic organisms, can make an awkwardness in the resistant mechanism, inciting more inflammation. It additionally makes the gut be progressively flawed, permitting inadequately stomach related nourishment section into the body where the insusceptible mechanism can experience it, creating more sustenance hypersensitivities and inflammation.

3. Adrenal weariness or adrenal weakness - adrenals are your pressure organs. They help your body manage worry alongside numerous different capacities including control circulatory strain, direct

glucose, help with hormone balance, give you vitality, drive and inspiration, they are additionally your body's wellspring of corticosteroids. Corticosteroids are amazing enemy of inflammatories. They are here and there given as a medication to address incendiary conditions as prednisone or corticosteroid puffers or nasal splashes. Supporting your adrenal organs can fix the body's capacity to make its own corticosteroids, reducing the requirement for outside intake.

4. Lack of vitamin C and vitamin B6 - both are normal enemies of histamines. And when they get exhausted you will be increasingly inclined to hypersensitivities and the inflammation related with it.

5. Lack of Omega 3 unsaturated fats - Our diets will in general be overwhelming in Omega 6 unsaturated fats and proportionately light in Omega 3's. The most productive approach to get omega 3's is from fish oil, either through expending fish 2-3 times each week or by enhancing with fish oil.

6. Obesity - Aside from the way that being overweight puts an additional strain on the joints, ligaments and tendons which can incite inflammation of the joints, ligaments or tendons, being overweight itself causes a constant, foundational inflammation.

This inflammation has been connected to the improvement of insulin obstruction and type II diabetes.

Presently you can smother inflammation utilizing anti- inflammatory prescriptions, for example, NSAIDs or prednisone, yet these are regularly joined by huge dangers and reactions, for example, draining stomach ulcers, expanded danger of heart assault or stroke and osteoporosis. They likewise don't address the basic cause for the inflammation. Fixing the basic cause assuages side effects on a progressively lasting premise, without the symptoms and enables your body to recuperate.

Step by step instructions to Reduce Inflammation in the Body Requires Your Attention

You're savvy to think about how to decrease inflammation in the body. What's more, significantly more astute to proceed to do it. All things considered, inflammation is the number cause for death. Time magazine called it "the Silent Killer" and specialists concur, constant inflammation is the hidden explanation behind for all intents and purposes each savage disease you can consider.

Alright, so you realize you have to do it. How?

The means are basic, however difficult. It will require some move in your reasoning. Some way of life changes. In any case, is certifiably not a more drawn out, more beneficial life justified, despite all the trouble?

Basic to decreasing your inflammation is your diet and exercise. In case you're eating a useless diet loaded up with refined flours and sugars, you're making inflammation in your body. At any rate restorative research demonstrates that is what's valid for the vast majority.

The manifestations of inflammation, swelling, redness and throbbing can be occurring inside your body without you notwithstanding knowing it. They're a sign your invulnerable mechanism is lopsided.

Supplanting undesirable foods with a lot of foods grown from the ground and get ordinary exercise will reduce inflammation for some individuals.

And when you presume a nourishment hypersensitivity/affectability you can remove the potential foods for three (3) months and check whether that makes a difference. A few specialists prescribe the "Base Diet" where you just eat fish, meat, vegetables and organic products for a month. The thought is you're not eating any cutting edge processed foods including grains. For some, this might be your answer.

Is it safe to say that you are Interested in Reducing Inflammation?

Decreasing inflammation is presumably the most significant dietary advance anybody can take. It is a two-stage process that isn't troublesome. Be that as it may, the arrangement must be reliable and when you need your wellbeing to be steady.

Inflammation is the thing that happens when your insusceptible mechanism escapes balance. A significant number of the present greatest wellbeing concerns are connected to inflammation of the body - malignant growth, coronary illness, stomach related mechanism issues and cerebrum related issues.

On one hand, this lopsidedness is brought about by an excess of white breads, vegetable oils, dairy items and processed foods. Then again, the normal Westerner is just not getting enough of the omega 3 basic unsaturated fats found in fish oil.

Omega 3s are a characteristic anti-inflammatory that help a solid body do what can do. That is battling sickness or outside contaminants without over responding.

For example, specific types of joint pain are just inflammatory joints. The body has sent too many white platelets and synthetic substances to the joint zone. The swelling causes pain and firmness. Lessening inflammation with omega 3s likewise reduces the weight and can reestablish versatility.

Here is the issue. Over 90% of us don't get enough omega 3s. Indeed, we are off by a long shot. The FDA and others accept that 2-3 grams of fish oil omega 3s every day are helpful for keeping up a sound grown-ups safe mechanism. The FDA additionally suggests a limit of two servings of fish for each week. Different specialists think even that is excessively.

This is the cause the fish oil supplement market is developing so quickly. It is incredibly hard to get even a base dose through our weight control plans.

An ongoing report from Finland pursued 21,000 individuals for around 11 years. Individuals who reliably took about 250mg of omega 3 fish oil enhancements had a half decrease in cardiovascular infection over the individuals who did not. Notice that reliably taking even little dosages was fruitful in reducing inflammation.

And when you are not kidding about lessening inflammation, your following stage is to examine the enhancement showcase. In nature, balance is everything. Begin the arrangement. You may get yourself more beneficial, less tranquilize subordinate and rationally progressively engaged. This type of way of life can be addictive [in a decent way].

Treatment For Inflammation - Diet Alone isn't Enough to Reduce Inflammation

In the event that you do any measure of finding out about medications for inflammation, you will discover heaps of exhortation on dietary changes as a treatment for inflammation. This is for the most part a word of wisdom.

In any case, in the event that you need to reduce inflammation, you should accomplish more than roll out a couple of improvements to your diet. While the suggested dietary changes are great and for the most part substantial, there is one extra thing that you have to totally reduce inflammation.

Myth #1: Reducing awful fats is sufficient...

Kindly don't misunderstand me - decreasing the awful fats in your diet is extraordinary guidance. In any case, if exhortation that you read persuades this is everything necessary, you are being deluded. Possibly not deliberately, yet this isn't the long and short of it.

Myth #2: Exercise and weight reduction is the key...

Once more, these are generally excellent things. We all ought to get a lot of activity and monitor our weight. Yet, in the event that you are persuaded this is the main treatment for inflammation, there is one extra thing that you should comprehend to lessen inflammation.

There is something many refer to as " Inflammation Syndrome" and it impacts your typical inflammation reaction. Inflammation Syndrome is a perpetual condition that changes your typical inflammation reaction to damage or injury. Incessant inflammation is a period bomb and incredibly risky to your long term wellbeing.

Fundamental inflammation is a noteworthy inconspicuous issue in most of the world. It is additionally called "quiet inflammation " since it is sub- intense. As it were, it's inconspicuous and flies under the radar. However, it is in charge of an enormous host of chronic conditions.

Fortunately ,there are some straightforward answers. You can discover long term alleviation and decrease inflammation that will demolish your wellbeing. Also, it's anything but difficult to do!

The Best Diet to Reduce Inflammation in the Body

So, you're searching for an diet to lessen inflammation in the body - they do exist. Be that as it may, do you know what the best diet is?

Whatever the diet, in the event that it has a high omega 3 unsaturated fat substance and a low measure of omega 6s, it will undoubtedly be powerful. Omega 6s give our body inflammation while omega 3 contains anti- inflammatory properties.

It is significant that we do get four-fold the amount of omega 6 than omega 3 in our diet. Be that as it may, as of late, this proportion has developed to be lopsided.

Rather than being 4:1, we end up with a proportion of 20:1 or 40:1 between omega 6 and omega 3. This is the because our diets need little omega 6 and more omega 3 - to adjust this proportion. Hence, we have to locate the best source of omega 3, as this will result in:

The Best Diet to Reduce Inflammation in the Body

The most normally rich source in omega 3 is fish. Greasy fish, like hoki, sardines, mackerel, salmon, and trout, contain large amounts of DHA and EPA, the two basic unsaturated fats.

Be that as it may, our waters are dirtied. This implies that the fish we eat for the most part contains unsafe poisons like mercury, lead, arsenic, dioxins and PCBs.

These are harmful to our wellbeing and subsequently ought to be avoided. At that point, how would we get the omega 3 from fish in the purest way possible?

A fish supplement is the most ideal approach to reduce inflammation in the body. They can be decontaminated to be powerful and safe.

The best cleansing procedure is called atomic refining. Pay special attention to this term in the event that you may want to research further.

A Diet to Reduce Inflammation in the Body -Yes, You Have Control

With all the inflammation, it's no big surprise such huge numbers of individuals are searching for a diet to lessen inflammation in the body. That is to say, specialists presently accept the fact that most, if not all, illnesses start with endless inflammation. What's more, you definitely know there's a rash of diseases, joint pain and auto invulnerable issue like lupus. Different investigations demonstrate that the hidden cause of each of these is inflammation.

A study found a connection among inflammation and disease. What's more, others have found connects to diabetes, asthma, hypersensitivities, and other ailments you can name. Luckily, you can help to prevent such. Exercise, rest, and an inspirational disposition will all assist in lessening inflammation; so will dietary changes.

Flavors and Herbs

Rosemary, turmeric and ginger all have anti- inflammatory properties. Actually, ginger has been perceived as a characteristic inflammation reducer for thousands of years. In this way, add more to your fish and chicken.

Fish

As it relates to fish, it's perhaps the best food to incorporate into your diet to decrease inflammation. Fish are rich in omega 3 unsaturated fats, which are important for inflammation decrease. That is the reason your PCP proposes you eat more fish or take fish oil supplements. Fish is rich in DHA and EPA which are building hinders for your mind, so they ensure retention or improvement in memory. The EPA keeps your state of mind adjusted so you remain increasingly positive.

That is the reason fish oil enhancements are so well known. They're advantageous, economical and can be filtered. Eating fish alone will give you about 30% of the omega 3 unsaturated fats you need. A decent quality fish oil supplement can give you 60% or more.

And when you pick an enhancement, make sure you get one with abnormal amounts of DHA and EPA. You likewise need to ensure they're sanitized utilizing a sub-atomic refining process. No compelling cause to ingest mercury and different poisons with your enhancements!

Best Natural Remedy for Inflammation - Reduce Inflammation In Your Body With Omega 3 Fish Oil

Is it true that you are searching for a successful characteristic solution for inflammation? When indeed, at that point, you have to begin taking omega 3 fish oil supplements. Omega 3 is a fundamental supplement that our bodies need to work ideally; tragically the human body does not contain what is expected to make it. Along these lines, we can just get it from our foods and by supplementation.

Inflammation is a guarded system utilized by the human body to fend off illnesses; along these lines, it is a characteristic event. In any case, a lot of it in your body, prompts genuine medical issues like coronary illness, eye issue, joint pain and malignant growth; truth be told, it may be considered the dominant part of ailments are brought about by incessant inflammation.

Utilizing a characteristic solution for inflammation, for example, omega 3 fish oil is superior to anything taking NSAIDs like Aspirin;

the greater part of the NSAIDs have negative symptoms since they contain synthetic compounds that are unsafe for your body. Omega 3 contains DHA unsaturated fat, which is transformed into an amazing anti-inflammation operator known as Resolvin D2.

In this way, and when you truly need a viable characteristic solution for inflammation, you should search for a fish oil supplement that contains high measure of DHA; the suggested least amount is 250 mg of DHA in a 1000 mg case.

DHA likewise lifts cerebrum capacities, for example, learning, focus and memory; henceforth, it forestalls dementia and improves the states of those with other mind related issues like discouragement, ADD and mental imbalance.

The greater part of the omega 3 fish oil supplements available contain poisons, for example, mercury and PCBs; in this way, guarantee you purchase a brand that is purged by atomic refining. That is the main way you can make sure that you are taking unadulterated and safe oil.

Lessen Inflammation in Two Steps

Inflammation in our body can cause:

- Acne, Eczema, Rosacea

- Food hypersensitivities and prejudices
- Digestive issues: IBS, colitis, Crohn's infection, Candida
- Chronic weariness, Fibromyalgia, General absence of vitality
- Brain mist, Lack of focus, Depression
- Attention shortage issue, Poor learning and osmosis
- Sinus issues, Chest diseases, Asthma
- Dental issues, Gum ailment
- Joint pain, Back pain, Muscle throbs, Lupus, Arthritis
- Thyroid brokenness
- Insomnia
- Weight gain, Obesity
- And substantially more...

Given the list above (which is in no way, shape or form complete), it makes sense that by controlling the incendiary reaction in the body and reducing inflammation, we can improve an incredible nature essentially. Consider multi day where your brain is clear, you have huge amounts of vitality, your stomach feels light, your skin is gleaming, you are expressive and certain, free of pain, and you have a feeling that you can overcome the world; that is not unattainable. It could be your existence once you are equipped with knowledge and obviously inspiration to accomplish a more joyful variant of yourself.

To control inflammation, we have to know what's causing it in any case. Though the components adding to inflammation appear to be intricate, the fundamental interesting points are stomach related wellbeing and emotional well-being.

Inflammation can be brought about by:

1. Poor absorption, digestion and end
2. Mental and emotional pressure

The cerebrum gut association

Critically, the primary driver of inflammation (stomach related and mental) are really related. Our cerebrum registers thoughts. Each time an idea is enlisted, the mind makes a substance (a neuropeptide) that is discharged into the blood. The small digestive tract does the very same thing - it produces the equivalent neuropeptides, with the exception of it being in amounts multiple times more significantly contrasted with the cerebrum. The neuropeptides, once in the blood, work as a medication. When we engage happy thoughts (of appreciation, love, connectedness), we discharge upbeat synthetic substances (endorphins) from the mind and from the gut. These cheerful synthetics make us feel glad and furthermore increases various solid qualities. Then again, when we have troubling thoughts, the cerebrum and the gut make destructive synthetics which can turn on malignant growth qualities and trigger inflammation, in addition to other things.

What would you be able to do to decrease inflammation?

Right off the bat, deal with your feelings of anxiety:

1. Use reflection and supplication. Remember to indulge in food and water.
2. Laugh more, watch more comedies, and don't pay attention to yourself or life as well.
3. Don't immerse yourself with an excess of violence and "fate and despair" shown in the media.
4. Live with trustworthiness (lying or not satisfying your promises is in reality distressing, regardless of whether you deliberately acknowledge it or not).
5. Write an appreciation list day by day.
6. Exercise consistently.
7. Volunteer your time, ability, cash or some other asset you may have for the benefit of other people. Commitment is probably

the most noteworthy type of satisfaction and puts the body-mind in a healing state.

8. Consider BodyTalk or other type of treatment to help you in decreasing worry.

Furthermore, get it together and tidy up your gut.

You are what you think AND what you eat. The physical and the psychological go together, so you should address both. Here are a few things to support the stomach related mechanism and, accordingly, reduce the occurrence of inflammation:

1. Stay hydrated (this by the way additionally causes you to release emotions). Drink a glass of water 30 min before a meal - this can enable the stomach to process your food better (and you will likewise be processing your thoughts better, since the stomach meridian houses the cognizant personality).

2. Use flavors to support assimilation and cut down inflammation levels: turmeric (my top pick!), dark pepper, Cayenne pepper, cumin, fennel, coriander, ocean salt, Himalayan salt, ginger, cinnamon and cardamom are for the most part extraordinary when utilized with some restraint.

3. Think about including some Ayurvedic supplements: Trikatu (helps stomach assimilation); Neem (helps clean and reestablish the small digestive system, sanitizes blood and clears skin break out); Triphala (helps disposal from the internal organ, incredible for the eyes also); Boswellia (mends the coating of the small digestive tract and is great for decreasing inflammation).

4. Incorporate foods that help reestablish the stomach related capacities: Lemon, coconut oil, ghee, chia seeds, linseeds, green vegetables, spirulina, beetroot, kumara, probiotic (non-improved) yogurts and kefir, and slippery fish.

5. Eat organic product independently from different foods. Organic products, when joined with other nourishment, mature rapidly in the stomach and lead to gas, swelling, acid reflux, candida and inflammation.

6. Some vitamins and minerals are significant for stomach related just as for emotional wellness: Vitamin D, vitamin C, vitamin B complex, Zink. A decent probiotic supplement alongside basic unsaturated fats can help as well.

7. Avoid: espresso, liquor, sugar, processed foods, nourishment added substances, refined carbs, hazardous fats. These foods are genius incendiary.

8. Consider acquiring a customized nourishing counsel from a certified professional.

Four Effective Anti-Inflammatory Herbs to Reduce Inflammation

A few medications, steroids or herbs are known to have anti-inflammatory properties. In any case, what anti- inflammatory implies? Inflammation is an intricate response of the body to the hurtful stimulant as inflammations, harmed cells or pathogens. Animal attempts to shield itself from the stimulant, expels it and after that begins the recuperating procedure. This procedure is significant in light of the fact that injuries start to mend by virtue of this provocative response. Thus, those substances as referenced before has unique properties which speeds-up the recuperating procedure and hence, known as anti-inflammation.

At the point when inflammation starts, white platelets become dynamic, as their fundamental capacity is to fix and shield your life form from remote bodies, infections, microbes, and so forth. White platelets have exceptional synthetic substances, which go to the kindled part of the body and start to swell. In the event that the inflammation happens very close to the skin, that region winds up red in shading, warm and throbs, additionally blood stream increments. Pain is the most widely recognized indication of inflammation. In some cases, internal organs may get influenced excessively because of inflammation.

Valuable herbs: Usually medications are the most well-known while treating inflammation, yet herbs may likewise help you in an increasingly common and safe way. They reduce indications and make you feel much improved, likewise has extra helpful properties. So, we should now view the valuable herbs with anti-inflammation properties

1. Turmeric: This is probably the best herb which viably fix inflammation like joint pain, auto-safe issue and tendonitis. Be that as it may, it won't work in a compelling way in the event that you are utilizing drugs. The greater part of the home-grown cures needs time. Be cautious and don't utilize turmeric regularly as it might cause indigestion. Pregnant ladies initially ought to counsel the specialist in the event that they need to utilize this herb.

2. Boswellia: It is broadly utilized in Ayurvedic drug. Boswellia soothes the undesirable manifestations of inflammation being rich in normal properties, which are like the mitigating drugs.

Interestingly, this herb does not bother the stomach related tract, and you can utilize it securely.

3. Ginger: Using ginger so as to ease the inflammation side effects is extremely valuable. This root is known to have numerous important properties. Likewise, with turmeric, you should sit tight for quite a while for observable impact, yet the consumption of ginger is extremely worth pausing.

4. Licorice: Also, you may have a go at utilizing this herb. It is exceptionally compelling. Simply have at the top of the priority list, that you ought not utilize it for exceptionally long as it might cause potassium misfortune and hypertension.

There are a lot increasingly home-grown cures, which can assist you with reducing inflammation. Arnica, fallen angels hook, bromelain, white willow, papaya should help you a great deal as well, however utilize every one of these herbs shrewdly and make sure that you are not sensitive to them, or and when you are sick with some other sickness, at that point better check with your primary care physician.

Keep up a solid way of life and eat legitimate foods and when you would prefer not to get into this condition. Likewise, treat every one of the maladies cautiously in order to maintain a strategic distance from further complexities

Lessening Inflammation - The Less Inflammation You Have Is Better for Your Health

Inflammation is a procedure inside our very own bodies which it uses to shield us from disease and damage. Like every one of these things throughout everyday life, a great deal of even an awesome thing can be terrible for us all. Any nutritionist or wellbeing mentor will educate you that the regular American diet is topped off with foods which increment inflammation inside our very own bodies. These incorporate sugars, processed grains and awful fats which are largely so common in most lousy foods. A few issues associated with such an diet are muscle or joint pain, asthma or sensitivities, higher pulse and glucose issues. This kind of diet additionally saps our vitality that you have to endure day by day.

A Healthier Diet to Lower Inflammation

And when you've been eating an diet high in sugars, at that point you will before long sense a ton of advantages from the appropriation of an diet comprising of foods that reduce inflammation. The accompanying types of foods will help you in such manner:

- Fruits

- Nuts
- Leafy green vegetables
- Fatty fish
- Fresh herbs and flavors

You may accomplish huge anti-inflammatory favorable circumstances from removing fricasseed foods, soft drinks, processed sugars and processed meats and joining these sound sustenance into your day by day diet. The fat in fish and nuts is a solid structure which additionally can help feed your brain. Foods grown from the ground highlight loads of fundamental minerals and vitamins that help keep you sound all in all while additionally battling inflammation particularly. At the point when combined with taking flavors and herbs, which are brimming with cancer prevention agents, you give your body precisely what it requires to feel alleviation from the hurts, throbs, absence of vitality and different markers of a horrible diet.

You'll Thank Yourself

Altering your diet is among the most troublesome prospects for some individuals. The vast majority of us catch wind of making New Year's goals which are left a long time after and wellness focus enrollments of those attempting to improve their wellbeing through exercise heading unused after two or three excursions. You need to do anything that's required to roll out this improvement that should happen without anyone else.

Teach yourself about foods on the web and through productions and eBooks, and furthermore consolidate gatherings on wellbeing related destinations and projects to connect with similar people that will help you to continue on. Should you will require an exercise center coach to keep you on course, at that point which may be the shrewdest venture you ever make. The mitigating included advantages of a nutritious diet will give you the vitality and wellbeing to deal with your day by day existence with a force which you probably won't be able to imagine right now. When you have this capacity to carry on with the existence you constantly needed, you won't ever need to come back to the manner in which you were.

CHAPTER FOUR

Classic Signs Of Inflammation

Inflammation is the body's organic reaction of endeavoring to secure itself. It means to expel unsafe boosts, for example, pathogens, harmed cells and inflammation; this is the initial step of the healing procedure.

Inflammation triggers a reaction from the invulnerable mechanism, at first inflammation is gainful for insurance however a ton of the time inflammation can prompt further inflammation which is terrible.

The five signs to pay special attention to for inflammation are pain, redness, warmth, swelling and harmed work!

Chronic Inflammation

Chronic inflammation is the point at which the underlying inflammation does not leave. It is never again a healing reaction however increasingly a marker that something isn't right. Probably the greatest cause for incessant sickness originates from the nearness of 'perpetual incendiary status'. Ceaseless inflammation is long term and can keep going for a considerable length of time or even years!

It is imperative to do all that you can to anticipate inflammation so you don't arrive at this stage.

The provocative procedure is in charge of the indications and long term harm and connected with oxidative pressure.

Oxidative pressure happens when there are an excessive number of poisons for the body to manage, the body then accordingly creates free radicals, and free radicals harm the films of the cells, crushing significant proteins, fats and DNA.

Goals of an unending inflammatory condition lies at the core of all endeavors to treat and anticipate these horrible sicknesses.

There are such a significant number of maladies and diseases which are brought about by interminable provocative conditions, for example,

- Cardiovascular disease
- Diabetes type2
- Metabolic disorder
- Fibromyalgia
- Chronic exhaustion

- Depression
- Alzheimer's disease
- Cancer
- Osteoarthritis
- Ibs
- obesity
- atherosclerosis

Inflammatory conditions are regularly multifaceted

Cortisol - (testosterone is an enemy of inflammatory) is the most dominant enemy of inflammatory and is discharged in light of pressure (dhea is additionally an endogenous anti-inflammatory).

What causes the inflammation in any case?

- Chronic contaminations
- Obesity
- Environmental poisons (nourishment, water and air)
- Physiological pressure
- Intensive/aerobic exercise

- Physical injury
- Age
- Autoimmune sickness Long term pressure exacerbates any inflammatory condition.

What are the solutions?

For individuals who experience the ill effects of interminable inflammation then it is imperative to reduce feelings of anxiety. Interminable inflammation is likewise much increasingly regular in overweight people, so one method for reducing the odds of incessant inflammation is to pursue the standard methodology to losing muscle to fat ratio (good dieting and exercise).

Individuals' diet should be improved to guarantee they are eating the majority of the essential vitamins and supplements and evading trans-fats and saturated fats. Eating herbs and flavors, for example, turmeric, garlic, onions and a lot more are connected with lessening levels of inflammation. The anti-inflammatory mixes found in these herbs and flavors give wellbeing from numerous points of view.

Guarantee to get a lot of rest and take enemies of oxidants. Numerous individuals who experience the ill effects of endless inflammation do so because of their way of life, so as to decrease their manifestations then the way of life should be changed. Being overweight is condition of incessant inflammation, so battling the fat will battle inflammation simultaneously!

As per the most recent restorative hypothesis, ceaseless inflammation is the main driver of pretty much every infection endured by people. It's hard to believe, but it's true. Numerous specialists accept diligent, low-level inflammation prepares for unending illness, including those we normally experience late throughout everyday life, for example joint pain, heart and kidney illness, and disease.

As a part of our safe reaction system, inflammation happens when the body is battling germs that enter the body through an assortment of ways, for example damage or inhaling. When you experience redness, swelling, warmth, disease, and pain from an assortment of infirmities, it's an indication of inflammation. Regularly, the inflammation leaves when the body has vanquished the disease or damage, however and when the body neglects to close off the inflammation procedure, an increasingly genuine condition can happen.

It is commonly perceived that heart assaults happen when the veins become stopped up with "plaque" (what we more often than not allude to as the awful LDL cholesterol) that is kept on the vessel dividers. This awful cholesterol likewise gets inserted inside supply routes and our invulnerable mechanism "assaults" it. Persevering inflammation in the veins can in the end cause plaque to blast. Presently numerous specialists utilize a basic blood test for inflammation called CRP (short for C-receptive Protein) to help survey an individual's cardiovascular hazard. CRP is a list of inflammation in the supply routes and the CRP increments as inflammation increments. For instance, test have demonstrated that moderately aged men with high CRP levels in their blood were multiple times bound to endure a heart assault in the following 6 years than men with typical levels. Therapeutic specialists state that a CRP of 3.0 mg/L or higher triples your heart assault hazard. Individuals with CRP under 0.5 mg/L once in a while have heart assaults.

Fortunately, we can plan something for decrease the dangers of constant inflammation, including getting in shape, practicing routinely, and eating the correct diet. As indicated by the Center for Human Nutrition at Johns Hopkins School of Public Health, a few diets can cause inflammation while others can reduce it. Diets that are rich in leafy foods, and diets that offer heaps of Omega-3 unsaturated fats, (for example, salmon, fish, mackerel, and pecans) are ideal. Further, an diet of such foods has been demonstrated to be instrumental in weight decrease and lowering CRP and insulin opposition.

You can likewise take solution or over the counter NSAIDs (non-steroidal anti-inflammatory medications, for example, Vioxx, Celebrex, and Bextra), which reduce inflammation however can have perilous symptoms. While these medications are successful COX-2 inhibitors, the hazardous symptoms from delayed continuous use, (for example, gastro- intestinal discharge and kidney and liver disappointment) make them both perilous and dubious. One has just to peruse the writing created by the organizations producing these medications to realize how hazardous they are. Indeed, in the United States in the year 2000, additional individuals passed on from the difficulties of NSAIDs than kicked the bucket from AIDS! Further, Vioxx was as of late pulled back from the commercial center since it caused heart assaults.

Inflammation is "one of the troublemakers." You have to get it leveled out, however don't hop from the "skillet into the fire" by treating your condition with a "badder person." Eat right, practice normally, have your blood work done once per year, and tune in to your primary care physician's recommendation. May I likewise recommend you locate a characteristic nourishment supplement to treat your inflammation, instead of simply going after the pill bottle?

How Inflammation Triggers Diabetes - And Anti-Inflammatory Tips to Live By

Inflammation is rising as a key factor hidden the advancement of type 2 diabetes, and it's one that numerous individuals have not known about. A typical and totally regular body reaction, inflammation is a procedure by which your white platelets and body synthetic concoctions shield you from microscopic organisms, infections and disease.

You can recognize intense inflammation in your body by redness, warmth, swelling, and pain at the site of damage. These are signs that your body is effectively battling a disease.

Be that as it may, under numerous conditions - regularly because of way of life factors or an over- responsive insusceptible mechanism - inflammation can end up perpetual, prompting a second-rate condition of decay in your body. For this situation, inflammation causes no ostensibly side effects despite the fact that it might make harm your system, which is the cause of what is otherwise called "quiet" inflammation.

Constant "quiet" inflammation isn't just involved in endless infections like coronary illness, malignant growth, Alzheimer's disease and rheumatoid joint inflammation, yet in addition in type 2 diabetes.

Inflammation has all the earmarks of being complicatedly connected to the improvement of type 2 diabetes. White platelets called macrophages trigger inflammation as a component of your safe reaction. Macrophages additionally discharge cell-flagging synthetic concoctions called cytokines, which cause cells to move toward becoming insulin safe, a condition wherein your body has lost the capacity to use insulin fittingly, and type 2 diabetes frequently pursues.

In individuals who are fat, findings demonstrate that macrophages move into fat tissue where they discharge cytokines and meddle with the cells' capacity to utilize insulin properly. This is an imaginable motivation behind why individuals who are overweight or corpulent are at an expanded danger of creating type 2 diabetes.

Truth be told, it's broadly realized that obesity adds to a condition of second rate "silent" inflammation just as insulin opposition. Notwithstanding, stoutness isn't the main provocative express that can trigger insulin obstruction.

Other provocative ailments like rheumatoid joint pain, hepatitis C and inflammatory lung ailments are likewise connected to an expanded danger of diabetes, which recommends that not exclusively may type 2 diabetes be an incendiary ailment too, however inflammation may likewise be to be faulted for why heftiness triggers insulin opposition and diabetes.

Basically, the area of the inflammation or incendiary cytokines in your body will direct what wellbeing condition or indications create. For example, inflammation in your cerebrum may prompt Alzheimer's, inflammation in your joints can prompt joint inflammation, and far reaching fundamental inflammation can prompt malignant growth, fibromyalgia and then some.

Separate research has likewise demonstrated that a protein called Fox01 invigorates macrophages and the creation of cytokines called interleukin-1 beta (IL-1B), which lead to insulin resistance. Insulin commonly represses Fox01, which implies that when your phones are never again touchy to insulin, Fox01 can trigger inflammation unchecked.

It's an unpredictable cycle, be that as it may, as an excessive amount of insulin is additionally a marker for inflammation. This is the cause a fasting insulin blood test, ordinarily used to screen for diabetes, can be a marker for inflammation; higher insulin levels regularly mean you have higher inflammation levels.

Obviously, corpulence is just one factor that is related with quiet inflammation in your body. It's possible, and very normal, to have unending inflammation regardless of whether you're not overweight or large, and this is regularly because of way of life factors.

Your Diet and Your Lifestyle Habits Can Increase Inflammation, Too

Numerous variables can animate constant inflammation in your body, including:

1. Overweight and stoutness
2. Unhealthy diet
3. Poorly controlled diabetes
4. Lack of activity
5. Gum sickness
6. Smoking
7. Stress
8. Long-term contaminations

You will see that numerous things on this rundown - unfortunate diet, absence of activity, gum illness - additionally increment your type 2 diabetes hazard, so in the event that you need to maintain a strategic distance from diabetes, it's critical to find a way to lessen the inflammation in your body.

This incorporates:

- Avoiding expert incendiary foods. The accompanying diets may add to foundational inflammation: trans fats (found in mostly hydrogenated vegetable oil), fried foods, sugar, bread and other refined carbs, soft drink, liquor, and polyunsaturated vegetable oils.

- Eating a lot of anti-inflammatory foods. Foods that help lessen inflammation incorporate crisp leafy foods, and wild-got fish (for the omega-3 fats).

- Exercising

- Quitting smoking

- Reducing worry in your life

- Considering certain anti-inflammatory herbs and flavors, for example, turmeric, ginger and boswellia.

- It's critical to downplay endless inflammation in your body to decrease your danger of type 2 diabetes as well as various other ceaseless ailments.

How would you know whether you have endless inflammation?

The C-Reactive Protein (CRP) test is the most widely recognized test used to distinguish inflammation; it quantifies a protein in your body that increments during foundational inflammation. In one examination, ladies with raised CRP levels were observed to be about multiple times bound to create diabetes than those with lower levels - and even subsequent to modifying for other hazard factors, the hazard was still more than multiple times as high.[4]

In any case, regardless of whether you realize you have raised CRP levels or not, it's a smart thought to make the strides above to decrease inflammation in your body. We all are affected by inflammation to changing degrees, and the best choice to keep the ceaseless, diabetes-connected type away is to lead a solid way of life as portrayed previously.

The Inflammation-Diabetes Connection

Inflammation is the body's response to disease or damage. Exemplary indications of inflammation are redness, swelling and pain. Living in Minnesota the model I consider is a mosquito nibble, where you feel almost no pain however you get the inflammation redness, swelling and tingling. That is a conspicuous incendiary response that is transitory.

Ever had a sinusitis? In the event that you go to the specialist you will be determined to have sinusitis. Any therapeutic determination that finishes with "itis" signifies inflammation. So, sinusitis essentially implies inflammation of the sinuses.

What does inflammation have to do with diabetes?

Diabetes and numerous perpetual medical issues are a state of inflammation, yet the unnerving part is that the inflammation is covered up. This concealed inflammation can begin path before you realize you have diabetes. You feel no pain until it has caused intricacies that occasionally are not reversible.

Inflammation prompts insulin opposition, which means your body needs to deliver more insulin to keep blood sugars typical. At the point where your body can never again keep up, blood sugars begin to run higher than typical all the more regularly. In the long run you may feel side effects however many don't feel any unique until blood sugars are during the 300s... multiple times the ordinary level.

What Causes Inflammation in our body?

There are numerous things that can cause the shrouded inflammation. Our condition, stress, dormancy, nourishment hypersensitivities or sensitivities, other wellbeing conditions and. The purpose behind this article… our diet. Our quick paced current world methods we are presented to progressively unsafe synthetic concoctions, we have more pressure, we sit a lot at a work area or before a screen, and we eat unreasonably many processed foods.

How Might You Reduce Your Level of Inflammation?

Begin "de-preparing" your diet. That implies eat less bundled diets and all the more whole natural products, vegetables and whole grains. It implies less eating out and all the more cooking at home. Sounds straightforward, yet it's definitely not. Changing the manner in which we eat requires some serious energy, arranging and adapting better approaches for cooking and trying new foods.

Where do I Start?

Consider these 3 changes in your diet to begin anti- inflammatory eating:

1. De-processing your diet.

Consider what you can do to settle on your suppers and nibble decisions not so much processed but rather more new sustenance. For instance, and when you are eating canned soups, at that point begin making your very own in bigger groups and stop thinking of fast suppers. In the event that you purchase treats, begin making custom ones. Set a standard for how frequently seven days you can eat out and begin preparing more suppers at home. These are only a couple of recommendations to start you off.

2. Eat progressively anti-inflammatory foods.

Your best source is fish, for example, salmon or fish or different foods high in omega-3, for example, flax dinner. Other anti-inflammatory foods incorporate whole grains, crisp leafy foods, and nuts.

3. Eat more fiber.

Once more, whole grains, natural products, veggies and nuts are your best decisions. Rather than cold oat, pasta or moment rice, attempt some less processed grains, for example, steel cut oats, grain, or dark colored rice. Remember to likewise drink more water as you increment fiber.

It is safe to say that you are Suffering from Chronic Inflammation?

In the event that you're eating a purported current diet, at that point you presumably have incessant inflammation. Foods like sugar, refined flours, soda pops and trans fats are generally causes for inflammation. These foods are generally late augmentations to individuals' weight control plans. The human body isn't adjusted to handling these new kinds of diets, so does not endure them well.

Perpetual Inflammation Symptoms

The issue is that there are frequently no undeniable indications of constant inflammation, or what signs there are we put down to some other causative factor.

That doesn't mean unending inflammation is absent in the body. An ever-increasing number of studies are demonstrating that it is one of the causes for various infections, including coronary illness, pancreatitis, diabetes, fibromyalgia, malignancy, metabolic disorder, incessant weakness disorder, and some more. The ceaseless inflammation in the body stresses it, permitting a dependable balance for different issues.

Being overweight is additionally a noteworthy concern and adds to numerous medical issues. The cutting edge diet isn't just causing unending inflammation, its adding crawls to our waistline. Those additional pounds cause additional inconvenience.

The Modern Diet Is Killing Us

The new diets we've added to our diet are causing issues. A portion of these professional incendiary foods incorporate sugar, soft drink, liquor, and bread made with refined flours.

Likewise, except if you've been living in seclusion, you've caught wind of the issues with trans fats, which are found in many snacks, fricasseed foods, wafers, confections, processed products, treats, vegetable shortening, a few margarines, plate of mixed greens dressings and numerous other processed foods. These are found in numerous foods we purchase in the market, or devour at cafés, and trans fats are known to increment foundational inflammation.

There are additionally synthetic substances in numerous foods that we truly have no clue what long term impact they will have on our wellbeing. Too many arranged foods are to a greater extent a compound mixture than a healthy sustenance.

So if these sustenance are demolishing our wellbeing, what can be done?

Attempt an Anti-inflammation Diet

Clearly, the basic response to the issue is to change our diet. For some individuals, in any case, that basic answer isn't anything but difficult to actualize. It requires a move in intuition, in what foods we purchase and how we plan them, and what foods we eat when eating out.

Perusing marks is significant. In the event that you've never tried to look at the names on sustenance, there's no time like the present to begin doing it! Search for fixings known to be issues, particularly trans fats.

Abstain from eating such huge numbers of processed foods. Rather, settle on whole foods, as near their characteristic state as could be expected under the circumstances, as the premise of your sound diet. Whole foods are wellbeing diet!

Improving Your Diet

It might all appear to be overpowering to make such a great deal of changes to your diet. And when it does, consider making tiny strides. Make changes in your diet a little at once, slowly improving it step by step.

Inflammation and Disease

There is a procedure in the body that is presently accepted by therapeutic specialists to be engaged with all realized sickness forms from coronary illness to malignant growth to Alzheimer's ailment -

inflammation. The majority of you will have encountered inflammation previously. Have you at any point got a cut on your finger? It got red and swollen, it might have drained a little and it was surely hot and excruciating - all the great indications of inflammation. Presently, inflammation is really an ordinary reaction to damage this way and it serves us well. It eliminates microscopic organisms, parasites and infections that attempt to attack us, and this inflammation keeps us alive. This kind of inflammation more often than not shows a 100 overlap increment in insusceptible mechanism markers, for example, white platelets and cytokines like IL-6, TNF alpha, or C receptive protein (CRP).

Anyway, there is another, darker inflammatory reaction that occurs in the body - what Dr Barry Sears calls "Quiet Inflammation". This type of inflammation doesn't inspire the pain, swelling, redness and warmth related with exemplary inflammation and may just show a 4-5 crease increment in invulnerable mechanism markers - so can regularly be difficult to distinguish. It can take years or even a long time to create and gradually harms DNA and prompts sickness. Sadly, present day drugs aren't truly adept at treating this kind of quiet inflammation. It is the consequence of poor way of life decisions and changing way of life and sustenance is a vastly improved strategy than utilizing anti-inflammatory drugs.

The causes for quiet inflammation are multi factorial:

- Over sustenance
- Excess liquor
- Poor diet
- Inactivity
- Pollution
- Poor rest
- Stress/misery
- Drug use

One of the essential wellsprings of quiet inflammation in the body is overabundance muscle to fat ratio. Fat isn't only an unattractive idle substance that sits on your stomach cushions or overhang. It doesn't simply fill in as a supply of vitality to be called upon when required for vitality. Fat is metabolic tissue that can make all way of things occur in your body. Fat cells become invaded with large amounts of safe cells that discharge inflammatory synthetic substances upsetting the take-up of sugar and copying of fat in liver cells adding to insulin obstruction, the beginning of type 2 diabetes and narrowing corridors. Fat cells discharge synthetic concoctions that coagulation your blood, increment your pulse and convert idle pressure hormones into dynamic pressure hormones and add to conditions, for example, hypertension, stroke, cardiovascular ailment and PCOS.

(Bring home point - lose muscle to fat ratio) Here is a short inflammation poll;

1. It is safe to say that you are overweight?
2. It is safe to say that you are taking cholesterol prescription?
3. It is safe to say that you are taking circulatory strain prescriptions?
4. Do you wake feeling sleepy every day?
5. Do you get sugar desires?
6. Do you experience the ill effects of weakness?
7. Dou you have weak nails?

And when you addressed YES to at least 3 inquiries you are likely experiencing Silent Inflammation. In the accompanying blog entries this feeble I'm going to disk inflammation as the course for heart assaults (not cholesterol), inflammation and circulatory strain, inflammation and malignant growth and inflammation and diabetes.

I'll likewise examine how to reduce inflammation through great nourishment, Stay posted.

Inflammation and coronary illness

Presently, this may be somewhat out there for some of you, particularly as we have been mentally programmed in to feeling that saturated fat and cholesterol squares courses and causes heart assaults. In any case, what analysts are presently discovering is that inflammation is maybe the real player here, not cholesterol.

As I referenced, the incendiary reaction gets activated whenever there is harm to the body. Tragically the body is under consistent low-level oxidative harm all the time from free radicals. These free radicals are terrible minimal insecure particles that fly around taking electrons from cells and for the most part causing ruin.

The body's guard to these free radicals are cell reinforcements; cancer prevention agents can securely give their electrons to the free radicals rendering them safe. The fundamental wellspring of cancer prevention agents in our body are shaped from the nourishment we eat, foods that contain amino acids and supplements, for example, vitamin A, vitamin C, vitamin E, zinc, selenium and numerous different mixes, for example, alpha lipoic acid, green tea concentrate and carotenes.

The exemplary coronary illness hypothesis looks similar to this:

- Too much cholesterol in the diet makes cholesterol be stored in the conduits, for example, the coronary corridors.
- Cholesterol kept in the coronary corridors causes narrowing or blocked courses and hello presto a heart assault.

An epic way to deal with coronary illness including inflammation resembles this:

- A terrible diet ailing in cell reinforcements prompts poor assurance from free radicals and oxidative harm.
- As cholesterol voyages however the veins it moves all through the vascular epithelial cells.
- Cholesterol is assaulted by free radicals and ends up harmed "oxidized cholesterol".
- Oxidised cholesterol isn't perceived by the by the invulnerable system which mounts a provocative response whereby resistant cells called macrophages go along and eat the oxidized cholesterol.

- The macrophage that has eaten the harmed cholesterol turns into a froth cell that is presently caught inside the epithelial cells that line the dividers of the corridors.

- As these froth cells develop, they cause narrowing of the corridor and can prompt decreased blood stream to the heart muscle.

- Hey presto a heart assault.

So, cholesterol just is by all accounts the honest observer of the oxidative harm brought about by an diet lacking cell reinforcements.

The Mediterranean diet

The Mediterranean diet is commonly viewed as the local diet of the occupants of Crete from between 1945 to 1970. It comprises of the accompanying diets:

- Abundant in plant foods(natural products, vegetables, heartbeats, beans and lentils, whole grains, nuts and seeds)
- Fresh natural product as the run of the mill day by day dessert
- Olive oil as the guideline wellspring of fat
- Saturated fat under 8% of all out calories

- Moderate dairy items for the most part cheddar and yogurt
- Moderate fish, sheep and poultry
- Low red meat
- Less than 4 eggs every week
- Moderate wine consumption 1-2 glasses every day
- Less than 2000 calories every day

This diet might be moderate to low in immersed fat, yet it is high in omega 3 fats, fiber and cancer prevention agents that help avoid inflammation.

Inflammation and hypertension

Silent inflammation adds to coronary illness as well as to hypertension or what is once in a while alluded to as hypertension. Presently, hypertension is to some degree an extraordinary illness as there aren't any perceptible manifestations in the beginning periods, so it's a smart thought to get your circulatory strain checked and do everything you can to keep it in the "typical" zone.

A considerable lot of you will have gone to the GP and had your circulatory strain estimated. You may have been informed that your circulatory strain is 120 more than 80 or 135 more than 90, however what do these number really mean?

At the point when your heart pulsates it powers blood out into the supply routes, which creates the principal number in a BP perusing. This number ought to be 120mmHg, which is viewed as typical, any higher than 140mmHg would be viewed as terrible, on the other hand if that number is too low it can likewise be awful. In any case if the courses were not solid or did not deliver some obstruction against the weight of the blood being siphoned out by the heart, the supply routes would tear open. This obstruction created by the conduits is the second number in a BP perusing. This number ought to be 80mmHg, which is viewed as typical, any higher that 90mmHg would be viewed as awful, alternately if that number is too low it can likewise be awful.

From logical research we can make estimations about your future dependent on your circulatory strain, as should be obvious the higher your pulse the shorter your future.

- BP of 130/90 = 67 ½ years
- BP of 140/95 = 62 ½ years
- BP of 150/100 = 55 years

The corridors are not simply static cylinders exhaustive which the blood streams, they can contract and enlarge contingent upon various factors, for example, stress, smoking and healthful status. In the event that a cylinder through which a liquid is moving river, the weight in that cylinder increments, on the other hand and when it broadens, the weight in the cylinder reduces much like what occurs in supply routes.

A significant number of you will have heard that in the event that you are overweight or eat an excess of salt you will have higher circulatory strain, and that to decrease pulse you have to lessen salt in the diet - genuine, however this isn't the main component at work here. Inflammation additionally assumes a major job in hypertension.

To comprehend this, we have to get familiar with a tad about vascular science (I can see your focus going out the window however hold on for me). The veins are fixed with cells considered endothelial cells that produce a large group of synthetic compounds that can tighten or enlarge your courses. One of the real vasodilators created by endothelial cells is nitric oxide, Nitric oxide essentially advises the veins to unwind and broaden, which will lessen pulse. What we cannot deny is that C-responsive protein (CRP) that provocative cytokine that I referenced before can reduce the generation of endothelial nitric oxide and increment inflammatory nitric oxide, prompting vasoconstriction and expanded pulse. Inflammation fundamentally eats up nitric oxide. We likewise realize that oxidative harm and free radicals decreases nitric oxide, and that hypertensive patients have reduced cancer prevention agents, for example, glutathione, superoxide dismutase, vitamin E, vitamin C, vitamin A, copper, and polyunsaturated fats.

So, there you have it - inflammation causes expanded circulatory strain.

One thing that has been appeared to decrease circulatory strain is something many refer to as the DASH (Dietary Approaches to Stop Hypertension) diet. The DASH diet is basically a low salt, low carb diet that is higher in protein and fundamental fats.

- Meat poultry and sleek fish 2-4 servings every day
- Vegetables 6-8 servings every day
- Fruits 4 servings every day
- Dried beans, seeds and nuts 1-2 servings per day
- Low fat dairy items 1-2 servings per day
- Cereals, grains and pasta 1-2 servings per day
- Fats and oils 4-5 servings per day (predominantly unsaturated fats like olive oil, fish oil, anyway some immersed fat is passable)
- Fiber - 50g per day (blend of solvent and insoluble fiber - may need to utilize a fiber supplement)

Again this diet is lower in incendiary foods and higher in cell reinforcements much like the Mediterranean diet (in actuality there are numerous likenesses).

Inflammation and malignant growth

A developing number of malignancy specialists are arriving at the resolution that malignant growth is fundamentally a provocative disease and that the more drawn out there is inflammation present in a tissue or an organ, the higher the danger of related carcinogenesis.

Epidemiological investigations gauge that almost fifteen percent (15%) of overall malignant growths are related with microbial contamination; this may incorporate cervical malignant growth and the HPV1 infection, gut malignant growth and provocative inside sickness because of bacterial dysbiosis and stomach disease auxiliary to H. Pylori contamination. These irresistible specialists are related with an inflammatory reaction in the body.

One way the resistant mechanism manages these trespassers is to discharge free radicals that slaughter the attacking infections and microbes. Be that as it may, these free radicals can likewise harm the DNA of sound cells. These cells either fix themselves or bite the dust. In the event that countless cells in a zone passes on auxiliary to contamination there is an incendiary intervened reaction that may prompt tumor development.

Numerous different malignant growths might be the consequence of long term endless disturbance and inflammation, for example, in smoking and lung disease or compound harmfulness (xenoestrogens) and bosom malignancy. By and by there is DNA harm, inflammation cell demise and tumor development.

In the long run these tumors are equipped for discharging provocative synthetic concoctions that can keep up their development, for example, by starting the development of fresh recruits' vessels that feed tumor development.

I'm not going to display a "hostile to disease" diet, yet I will recommend that sugar could be a contributing cause to malignant growths. Malignant growth adores sugar is an explanation that appears to be supported. Malignant growth cells seem to utilize a mix of a lot of sugar and explicit proteins to disregard cell directions to cease to exist and continue developing. Furthermore, we realize that individuals who expend more omega 3 fats, cell reinforcements and fiber experience the ill effects of malignancy. So, by eating a diet that is anti- inflammatory such an diet rich in sleek fish, products of the soil may shield you from malignant growth.

Inflammation and diabetes

Inflammation may likewise be a cause for type 2 diabetes. This type of diabetes is commonly viewed as the consequences of being overweight and from eating an excessive amount of sugar which makes the cells impervious with the impacts of insulin.

In any case, what may really be the cause is... inflammation!

I've just talked about how being overweight causes the arrival of an whole heap of incendiary synthetics that add to what is calls "silent inflammation ". Indeed, investigate on mice demonstrates that inflammation incited by safe cells called macrophages (similar cells that become froth cells and lead to blocked courses - and that are likewise moved in fat cells) prompts insulin obstruction and type 2 diabetes.

This exploration was done in mice that were hereditarily built to do not have a particular quality present in the insulin-creating cells of the pancreas.

These qualities are delicate to the chronic reaction brought about by macrophages and when these mice did not have the quality, they didn't create diabetes, notwithstanding when nourished an incredibly high-fat diet.

Presently this exploration was done in mice and applying it to people should be taken mindfully, anyway there is a decent contention to reduce inflammation to ensure the pancreas.

Other anti-inflammatory foods that can be valuable in shielding yourself from "quiet inflammation" include:

- Oily fish rich in omega 3 fats
- Ginger
- Garlic
- Turmeric
- Quercitin found in onions, broccoli, tea, wine and grapes.

Inflammation and Anti-Aging

Inflammation is to a limited extent a well-working insusceptible mechanism which invigorates a mind-boggling arrangement of concoction and cell exercises performed by the body in light of damage or anomalous incitement brought about by a physical, substance, or organic operator. We have all known about inflammation, felt its uncomfortability, and managed it in our standard ways. In any case, a significant number of us don't have the foggiest idea about that there is an immediate connection among inflammation and maturing. We don't know that free radicals inside our body are the offender of inflammation and factors in our consistently life trigger these free radicals that can disturb cell work. This article will help clarify that day by day inflammation supported over one's lifetime is the shrouded cause for maturing and sickness. It will look at the causes for inflammation and will offer chances, through diet and supplementation, to control these strange cell exercises, giving a sound age the board way of life.

Maturing is inescapable however how one ages is a decision. A few people appear to age well, looking more youthful than their genuine birth date; others seem, by all accounts, to be 10 years more seasoned than their sequential age. Our hereditary cosmetics decides how we age however there are different factors similarly as significant. Therapeutic intercession has broadened life expectancy. While the normal life expectancy in 1900 was roughly 46 to 48 years; today, people can hope to live into their eighties. However, how one lives these years and how well constant disease is kept under control, is profoundly subject to hostile to maturing factors.

The "free extreme hypothesis of maturing" looks at the components that effect our qualities and gives an establishment to how we age. In straightforward terms, the hypothesis clarifies how changes happen and how we can anticipate and defeat maturing issues that result from damage, disease, or DNA harm. The message is that free radicals inside the body are the fundamental driver of inflammation, bringing about illness. Control free extreme harm through dietary decisions and supplementation of cell reinforcements, and you control harm to DNA.

Free radicals are exceptionally charged iotas that are missing one electron, making them shaky. They enter our body through daylight, less than stellar diet, consumption of liquor, tobacco, airborne synthetics; even pressure and take an electron so as to increase concoction security. Most loved targets are unsaturated fats; cell layers which are rich in phospholipids; DNA and proteins. At the point when focused methodical cell procedures are supplanted by the articulate disarray of electron swapping that inevitably upsets cell work. Free radicals are viewed as the essential offenders in maturing on the grounds that they produce arbitrary radical change and deviation from a well-requested typical cell digestion. As a result, free radicals produce inflammation and day by day inflammation supported over a lifetime is the cause for maturing and sickness. Certain indications of inflammation incorporate swelling, heat, pain in joints, and redness. As we age, our guards decrease, and our tissues gather the finished results of oxidative harm. We see our skin is wrinkling or maybe we are collecting "age spots". Within our body, oxidative pressure harms key particles fundamental to our DNA, causing malignant growth, diabetes, coronary illness, poor course, and other age- related infections.

DNA is especially touchy to oxidative pressure. As electrons are stolen, they leave "pits" in the individual strands of DNA. Free radicals cause strands of DNA to split and erode. The subsequent scratches and strand breaks influence both working cells and undeveloped cells. Undifferentiated cell harm is incredibly pulverizing, since these cells are antecedents for a huge number of various types of cells found in the body. Since the significant job of foundational microorganisms is proliferation, harmed immature microorganisms influence future ages of every single working cell. Malignancy is one disease that relies upon DNA harm. A recognizable case of this is the numerous types of skin malignancy.

Inflammation is a noteworthy guarded instrument of the body's resistant mechanism. When a remote body is distinguished, the invulnerable mechanism reacts with inflammation, portrayed by redness, swelling, and pain at the site of contamination. Very similar things that trigger free radicals cause inflammation. Daylight, brown haze, airborne synthetic substances, horrible diet, liquor, medications, smoking, and stress are for the most part causes for inflammation. Intense inflammation happens because of damage or disease. For the most part inside a 24 to 48-hour time frame, this stage settle itself and recuperation procedure starts. Cell trash is expelled from the site of damage and sound substitution tissue develops. As we age, our cell reinforcement protections decrease, and the oxidative harm causes perpetual chronic conditions. This type of inflammation is increasingly drawn out. Free radicals, serious pressure, and natural operators don't react to safe assault. There is no recuperation procedure and serious pain and tissue harm happen. Beating these conditions and switching maturing relies upon effective DNA fix. Our inquiry is how might we help nature along a fix procedure for DNA and invert maturing? One path is through diet and supplementation. Another way is the manner by which you lead your life. The two methodologies are decisions.

Suitable diet, supplementation, and way of life decisions are basic to forestalling inflammation, killing free radicals, and advancing solid age the board. Among our decisions, there are acidic and soluble based foods. Diet should comprise of 80% soluble diets and 20% acidic foods. A rainbow determination of six servings of foods grown from the ground, natural at whatever point possible, can guarantee this immeasurably significant acid/basic parity lessening inflammation through furnishing the body with a huge number of cell reinforcements. Carrots, pumpkin, peppers, tomatoes, mangos, and papaya are generally orange and "red coded" and secure our qualities. Asparagus, broccoli, bok choy, onions, and mustard greens are 'green coded' and help improve cell supplements and detoxify our body. Blackberries, fruits, beets are purple and blue and reduce inflammation. Grain, mushrooms, tofu, and wild rice are tan and lessen insulin opposition and parity hormones. Herbs and flavors, for example, garlic, tumeric, cinnamon, curry, ginger, and cayenne help to kill free radicals.

By and large, meats, grains, nuts, and sugar are acidic and advance unfortunate free radicals. Meats ought to be unfenced, implying that they are free of hormones and anti-microbials. One ought to have an diet of ranch raised salmon, tilapia, flop and sardines and keep away from swordfish which is known to be high in mercury. Grain, quinoa, dark colored rice and wild rice are superb selections of grains. Nuts and seeds are essential to a balanced diet. Dark green vegetables, other vegetables, and red, yellow, orange, and green vegetables must be overwhelmed by every meal in order to adjust the important acidic foods which offer us the genuinely necessary protein, vitamins and minerals our body needs. We can further reduce inflammation with elevated amounts of antacid water intake, green tea and maintaining a strategic distance from sugar, vinegar, salt and corn syrup. More or less; stress lean natural protein, and join vegetable sources, eat specifically, stay away from sugary desserts, nitrates, nitrites, smoked meats, and trans-fats, watch segment sizes, don't eat on the run, and bite your sustenance. You ought to have five servings of leafy foods; ideally green and orange red shading choice. Drink a lot of fluids between dinners; no soft drink, eat suppers at ordinary occasions; don't eat late, and dodge processed diets. Reduce dairy consumption. We are the main species that expends another species milk!

Numerous anti-inflammatory enhancements are cancer prevention agents and help our body control free extreme harm. Superb multi vitamin/mineral complex is basic to a sound way of life. Folic acids, B vitamins, vitamins D, C, An, E, Boswella, Glucosamine- Chondroitin, curcumin, molecularly refined Omega 3 and 6 from virus water fish Tri-Methylglycine, CoQ Enzyme 10, R-Lipoic Acid, and Resveratrol are for the most part supplements that will hinder illness movement and reduce inflammation. Vitamins A, C, and E bring down the danger of coronary illness. They decrease inflammation and ensure against initiated oxidative harm. Those with diabetes can see improvement in "insulin activity". Green tea secures against estrogenic bosom disease. Vitamin D3 counteracts colon malignant growth and matured garlic averts harm to DNA and furthermore reduces inflammation. For the most part, by expanding detoxification, we free our groups of free radicals.

The consumption of the compound CoQ10 has critical results in controlling maturing. This enhancement counteracts oxidative harm to the cerebrum, upgrades expedient recuperation and cardiovascular capacity from heart assaults, and forestalls thyroid issue. Alpha-Lipoic acid improves sugar digestion, improves mind vitality and solid skeletal execution and "splashes" up free radicals inside the body.

Diet, supplementation, and learning are the key fixings to age the board. In any case, way of life changes totals the whole picture in advancing life expectancy. Research demonstrates that pressure starts significant changes in cell structure that lead to maturing ailments, especially those including inflammation and invulnerable capacity. Work towards disposing of pressure and you draw out life expectancy. Day by day exercise, supplication and reflection are additionally positive powers to fuse into one's life. Figure out how to be careful, build up an association with your God, and think "comprehensively". Lessen liquor consumption, help your stomach related procedure with probiotics, create legitimate disposal and reduction acidic foods. There is no enchantment projectile yet a longing for health turns into a way of life that comes bearing significant presents for an existence of feeling better and looking great. Genuine magnificence originates from inside. There are no alternate routes!

CHAPTER FIVE

Foods To Avoid

This anti-inflammation diet is a program used to anticipate and lessen the dangers of heart sicknesses. Around, a supper ought to be made out of 40% sugars, in addition to 30% protein and another 30% for sound fats. Suppers must be prepared of time. It is ideal to get ready at any rate 10 plans to abstain from eating a similar sustenance in excess of 5 times each week. However much as could reasonably be expected, eating as much products of the soil developed naturally is profoundly suggested. They contain up to multiple times more vitamins and minerals.

Additionally, choosing natural foods decrease your introduction to pesticides.

In following the counter inflammation diet, there is no restriction to the measure of food that you can devour. Here are some foods that you can eat:

1. Steamed vegetables are profoundly prescribed to improve the use and the accessibility of the sustenance supplements. This will

enable the body to begin fixing itself. Then again, eating crude vegetables ought to be done negligibly aside from when having plates of mixed greens. In any event one kind of green vegetable ought to be incorporated into the diet consistently.

2. Any vegetables can be eaten, however, tomatoes and potatoes ought to be kept away from until further notice. However much as could be expected, it is ideal to pick and eat generally vegetables that have low glycemic sugar, from 3- 6%. A few vegetables with 3% glycemic starch are asparagus, broccoli, celery, cucumber, lettuce, spinach, parsley, and watercress. Vegetables with 6% glycemic starch incorporate string beans, eggplant, leeks, red pepper, pumpkin, turnip and zucchini. Carrots, squash, green peas and artichokes have 15%, while yam has 20% glycemic starch.

3. It is fitting to just eat one to two (2) servings of organic products with the exception of citrus. What's more, if possible, it's ideal to have the organic product heated.

It might be not very simple to design nourishment for an adversary of inflammation diet, yet positive changes in the body will happen and results can be perceptible in weeks (4) to about a month and a half.

Decrease Inflammation Only By Choosing the Right Natural Food

Nourishment is the most ideal approach to improve any wellbeing condition, yet then again sustenance can aggravate it moreover. Decades ago food was no issue. We ate the food that was accessible and it didn't influence our wellbeing since it was all normal than. The assortment of nourishment and preparing has expanded and this is the place the issues begin. With regards to inflammation and joint inflammation related pain, choosing an inappropriate food can exacerbate it and disturb that circumstance considerably more.

Research has demonstrated that more than forty percent (40%) of the individuals around the globe are experiencing distinctive s ailments because of the type of diets they eat. What's more, a major level of them frequently don't think about the common anti- inflammatory foods that they ought to incorporate into their weight control plans. At the point when a specific ailment raises its appalling head there is a purpose for this; there was a trigger point for it to occur. For what cause are a few people increasingly powerless to contamination from a transferable infection than others, frequently only a typical virus? Have you seen a few people barely ever get anything as where others get any bug that is coasting about attracted like by an attractive field?

Immune System

Our body has a safe system which is in charge of dismissing any sickness that goes along, or it can open the entryway and giving it access. The resistant mechanism comprises of various capacities, for example, a body detoxification mechanism, the provocative and anti-inflammatory system. In the event that lopsidedness happens in any of those systems by not getting the correct supplements this will expand the danger of any disease including any type of malignant growth. The urgent point is if sustenance disappointment happens all the while any type of sickness is practically unavoidable.

Diets that cause inflammation

These are a portion of the provocative foods, an absolute necessity to maintain a strategic distance from:

- Refined sugar
- Any type of processed sugar
- Artificial sugars
- Any high glycemic starches
- Refined grains
- Vegetable oils

- Excessive liquor
- Processed financially raised meats
- Avoid trans fats and generally oils

This is the thing that you should know: Set diet plans don't work for everybody. There are in every case some who respond severely even to a decent and solid diet. Tune in to your body, it will tell you.

Here are a few recommendations of the best normal anti-inflammatory diets that you should change to.

Oils and fats

Omega 3 unsaturated fats are one of the significant supplements that have chilling off impacts for inflammation. Slick fish, for example, mackerel, fish, sardines, and salmon are rich in omega 3 unsaturated fats which has a solid impact in reducing inflammation.

For you to get these advantages, you ought to eat fish in any event 2 to 3 times each week. Similarly, as significant, you have to cook them solid. In the event that browning utilize just Coconut or Macadamia nut oil. A wellbeing study showed that eating fish 3-4 times each week could reduce the danger of coronary illness by up to thirty percent (30%) contrasted with the individuals who don't eat fish. This implies you ought to incorporate fish in your diet as a method for lessening inflammation. Olive oil: Just one tablespoon of olive oil every day has numerous medical advantages. It is useful for the heart, cholesterol and circulatory strain. As per medicinal science, additional virgin olive oil is probably the most beneficial sustenance we can add to our diet. This oil is great for joint pain sufferers due to a substance called oleuropein to cool inflammation and facilitating joint pain.

Dark Levy greens

Studies have demonstrated that dark green vegetable have vitamin E which frequently assumes a significant job in shielding the cells of the body from the star provocative atoms known as cytokines. A portion of the green veggies you ought to eat incorporate spinach, broccoli, collard green and kale. Cruciferous vegetables and dark greens likewise have higher convergences of minerals and vitamins, for example, iron, calcium, and infection battling phytochemicals when contrasted with those with lighter hued leaves. This too incorporates them among normal anti-inflammatory foods you can eat. Not to overlook ginger: Ginger is a viable pain reliever and decreases inflammation too.

Low fat dairy

Low fat dairy such unsweetened Greek yogurt has probiotics which can reduce inflammation of the gut. Foods rich in vitamin D and calcium, for example, skim milk and yogurt are useful for everybody since they help in the fortifying of bones and possibly other medical advantages. At whatever point possible, top up your vitamin D from the sun. Vitamin D has numerous other medical advantages, including for inflammation and joint pain. It would be ideal if you note that not all fats are equivalent. Our body needs fat however the correct ones.

Nuts

Nuts, for the most part almonds, are among the best regular anti-inflammatory foods that you ought to eat since they are rich in calcium, fiber, and vitamin E. Furthermore, pecans have high measures of the alpha- linolenic acid, which is an omega 3 that is important for fixing the harms brought about by inflammation. You ought to recollect that nuts (alongside green vegetable, whole grains and fish) structure the fundamental part of a Mediterranean diet that has been demonstrated to help reduce inflammation internally for six to seven weeks.

Green tea

Green tea is additionally among the characteristic subterranean insect incendiary foods which contain anti-inflammatory flavonoids that may help. Green tea likewise has numerous other medical advantages. In the event that you drink tea why not pick green tea? This unquestionably makes it another nourishment that you ought to incorporate into your diet to battle inflammation.

Sweet potato

Sweet potato is another ideal wellspring of fiber, beta carotene complex, carbs, manganese, vitamin C and B 6 which will reduce inflammation inside your body. Sweet potato has other medical advantages too – it reinforces bones, lifts your temperament, battles malignancy and improves vision.

Incorporate as much of the previously mentioned anti- inflammatory foods in your diet. Choose, however, many assortments possibly allowed. Being consistent, you will before long feel the advantage. The most significant advance to a more advantageous, pain free life is the change to a suitable diet.

Battling Inflammation with Food

In the event that you experience the ill effects of joint inflammation and joint pain, or constant infections like diabetes and coronary illness, you should realize that inflammation in the body can aggravate manifestations of such. Be that as it may, there are expectations.

Diet can help battle inflammation in your body. Actually, eating a diet rich in anti-inflammatory foods can likewise improve any hormone irregular characteristics, and can offer numerous different advantages like:

- Improved vitality
- Reduction in joint and muscle pain
- Less joint swelling
- Improved portability
- Improved processing with less swelling and gas
- Bowel normality
- Clearer thinking
- Reduction in migraines
- Better quality rest
- More stable dispositions

- An improvement of fasting glucose levels and lower lipid levels

Diets That Fight Inflammation (And Those That Don't)

Most importantly, and when you need to lessen inflammation in your body, you should maintain a strategic distance from:

- Refined sugars and grains like white flour, white rice and table sugar.

- Junk food and cheap food. They regularly contain awful fats (trans fats) that exacerbate inflammation.

- Foods that cause sensitivities like wheat, dairy, eggs can increase inflammation.

- Saturated fats. Changing to low fat dairy items and lean meat may help.

- Processed meats, for example, lunch meats, franks and frankfurters. They contain nitrites and sulphites that can advance inflammation.

- Too much Omega 6 fats - safflower, corn and sunflower oils.

To decrease inflammation in your body, do the following:

- Drink at least 6 to 8 glasses of water each day.

- Balance the Omega 6 in your diet with Omega 3. Use margarine and additional virgin olive oil.

- Eat an assortment of splendidly hued vegetables and natural products every day.

- Eat chicken, profound water fish, vegetables and beans more regularly than red meat.

- Eat seeds, nuts and their margarines. Ground flax, pumpkin seeds, just as sesame and sunflower seeds, are incredible decisions.

- Avoid seared food more often than not.

- Eat an assortment of grains other than wheat - quinoa, buckwheat, cereal, darker rice, millet.

- Avoid sugar - particularly table sugar. Extremely modest quantities of maple syrup, grain syrup, nectar or Stevia can be utilized when required.

Continuously utilize the 90/10 standard when choosing diets to battle inflammation: 90% of the time, adhere to the above rules; the other 10% of the time, cut yourself a little room to breathe. What's more, tune in to your body. And when your body has pain or any of different side effects recorded above, observe what you have eaten and lessen that food in your diet to check whether it has any kind of effect.

Mitigating Foods to Add to Your Diet

I don't understand what inflammation means? It's anything but an infection, despite the fact that disease can cause inflammation. All things considered, inflammation is the body's own safeguard endeavor to evacuate unsafe upgrades, for example, inflammations, harmed cells and so forth. This is when inflammation is attempting its recuperating procedure.

Inflammation is the principal sign when something destructive or bothering is influencing portions of our body. Everyone's body has an insusceptible mechanism and inflammation is a part of that. Inflammation is likewise a limited physical condition that results as a response to damage or disease, making portions of the body become swollen, blushed, painful and hot. Internal inflammation can occur because of eating of processed foods, fats and sugars.

Large amounts of inflammation can cause various wellbeing intricacies, for example, joint inflammation, joint pain, and harm to veins, among others. To battle this, it is significant you eat foods that are anti-inflammatory. Such diets are promptly accessible to add to your diet to control inflammation. Here are a portion of the diets and recommendations to help and keep hurtful inflammation under control. These are:

Whole Grains

With regards to whole grains it is better you expend your grains as whole grains and not refined or pasta. Research has demonstrated that whole grains contain a high measure of fiber which decreases the inflammatory markers in the blood known as C-responsive protein.

Dark Leafy Greens

Dark green vegetables, for example, spinach and kale have high centralizations of vitamin E and minerals, for example, calcium and iron. Studies demonstrate that vitamin E helps in shielding your body from harmful atoms known as cytokines. Moreover, dark green vegetables have a high measure of disease battling phytochemicals.

Fatty Fish

Sleek fish, for example, salmon and fish are diets that are mitigating as they contain high measures of omega 3 unsaturated fats. The unsaturated fats are known to help joint inflammation. So, ensure you get a lot of omega 3. Another significant fact about omega 3 is you should get it in your diet in light of the fact that the body can't make it inside its mechanism.

Soy

Soybeans contain isoflavones mixes which help the negative impacts of inflammation on joints. In any case, it is great you avoid vigorously processed soy items as they may contain added substances and additives. Rather, incorporate soymilk and soybeans into your normal diet.

Nuts

Nuts, for example, almonds and pecans are rich in vitamin E, calcium and fiber. All nuts are brimming with cell reinforcements which can help the body in fixing the harms brought about by inflammation.

Berries

Berries are low in fat and calories however rich in cell reinforcements. Their anti-inflammatory anthocyanins compound in them has numerous great characteristics. This keeps you from creating joint inflammation.

Green Tea

Green tea also has anti-inflammatory flavonoids; this reduces the beginning of inflammation and limits the danger of specific malignant growths. It shouldn't be thought little of for some, other medical advantages. It can reactivate skin cells causing skin to seem more splendid. Drink it consistently and utilize some nectar as a sweetener, rather than sugar itself.

Low Fat Dairy

Low fat dairy, for example, yogurt contains probiotics which can forestall inflammation. Moreover, dairy foods that are anti-inflammatory, for example, skim milk with high calcium and vitamin D are significant for everybody since separated from having anti-inflammatory properties, they reinforce your bones too.

Ginger and Garlic

Ginger and garlic are foods that are mitigating. Both are known to lower body inflammation, control glucose levels and help your body in battling certain diseases. Selenium and sulfur in garlic is a fundamental compound for a solid safe mechanism. It is additionally one of the top enemies of maturing foods you can eat.

Turmeric and Sweet Potato

Turmeric has common mitigating mixes called curcumin which is known to mood killer NF-kappa B protein that triggers the procedure of inflammation. Then again, sweet potato is a decent wellspring of fiber, vitamin B 6, vitamin C, complex sugars and better carotene.

These fixings help to mend inflammation in your body. These are some of numerous diet that are anti- inflammatory which can help you in joint aches and joint pain brought about by inflammation. Add them to your diet. Notwithstanding, decrease foods that are high in fats particularly trans fats and sugar as they can prod inflammation, joint pain, joint inflammation, and harm veins, among other related chronic conditions.

Making a couple of improvements will improve numerous things and can make you feel livelier and more invigorated than you have in quite a while, and will keep on doing so such as long as you remain with the progressions you made. This is the area many fail. At the point when things have improved, most return to a similar old path as in the past. Try not to attack your very own wellbeing; stick with what you are doing, the progressions you made, that made you feel much improved. Try not to return to the old ways of what you've done previously.

The Anti-Inflammatory Diet: How It Can Protect You from Disease

Inflammation is something worth being thankful for. It is the regular way your body reacts to dangers, for example, diseases or wounds. We have all observed inflammation at work when we have pain and redness at damage. We state it looks irritated, and it actually is, on the grounds that damage actuates the inflammatory reaction.

When is inflammation an issue?

At the point when inflammation goes on for significant time, we call it constant, and it can cause issues. Some basic causes for unending inflammation include sensitivities, immune system ailment, periodontal ailment, joint inflammation, and different illnesses that actuate the safe system after some time. Indeed, even being overweight is a cause, on the grounds that fat cells emit synthetic substances considered cytokines that trigger inflammation.

For what cause is it an issue?

Endless inflammation may harm the endothelial covering of corridors, which can prompt atherosclerosis and coronary illness. There is likewise proof that it adds to type 2 diabetes, Alzheimer's sickness and a developing number of other constant maladies that are basic in present day, western lifestyle.

What are the side effects?

The side effects of inflammation fluctuate with what is causing it. You may even have no manifestations by any means, as on account of being overweight. Here are a few instances of explicit sickness related side effects:

- Arthritis, rheumatoid joint pain (joint pain, firmness, swelling)
- Crohn's disease or ulcerative colitis (stomach pain and cramping, fever, loose bowels)
- Psoriasis or skin inflammation (redness)
- Allergies (respiratory manifestations, hives)

Increasingly unobtrusive, early markers of issues could incorporate cerebral pains, muscles pain, exhaustion, muscle firmness, queasiness, regurgitating, the runs or blockage, gas, stomach uneasiness and even emotional issues including depression. These could be identified with diet sensitivities and bigotries. The most well-known food bigotries incorporate dairy (lactose), wheat (gluten), yeast, soy, corn, eggs and even some counterfeit sugars.

How might you know whether you have constant inflammation in the event that you don't have indications or a conclusion?

You can see whether you have inflammation by having your C-receptive protein levels tested. The high affectability C-receptive protein is the favored marker of endless, poor quality inflammation.

What would it be advisable for me to do and when I have large amounts of C-responsive protein?

In the event that your C-receptive protein levels are high, you will initially need to converse with your primary care physician to see whether there is a hidden infection, sensitivity, immune system issue or another contributing disease. If not, being overweight could be the cause and weight reduction is your best line of defense. If you are a smoker, that could likewise be adding to the issue.

How do foods impact inflammation?

Inflammation can likewise be affected by the diet you eat. Research has demonstrated that specific foods trigger inflammation and others suppresses it.

A portion of the foods that are star incendiary include:

- Animal fats (corn-encouraged hamburger, dark meat and skin of poultry, pork, duck

- Hydrogenated fats (trans fat)

- Fried foods (browned in saturated, hydrogenated or polyunsaturated fats)

- Sweets (sugar, treats, treats, cakes, dessert, doughnuts, sweet drinks)

- Refined grains (white bread, pasta, and white rice)

- Processed diet (chips, saltines, fries, cold cuts, sausage, canned meats)

- Dairy items (particularly full fat milk, cheddar, harsh cream, cream cheddar, cream)

- Some individuals may likewise need to maintain a strategic distance from the nightshades (potatoes, tomatoes, eggplant, peppers)

Here are probably the best mitigating diet:

- Fatty fish, for example, salmon, sardines, herring, trout and fish (with omega 3 unsaturated fats)

- Grass sustained hamburger likewise contain some omega 3 fats (not at all like corn- nourished meat, generally saturated fats)
- Nuts and seeds (pecans, flaxseed, almonds)
- Monounsaturated fats (olive oil, canola oil, avocados), by supplanting polyunsaturated fats
- Turmeric (some portion of most curry dishes)
- Ginger, utilized in Asian cooking (additionally helps control sickness)
- Whole grains (with the exception of wheat, grain and rye and when you are gluten bigoted)

Foods that have high cell reinforcement levels likewise will in general decrease inflammation, perhaps by reducing the harm that invigorates inflammation. Cell reinforcements are productive in splendidly and obscurely shaded foods grown from the ground.

The absolute best wellsprings of cell reinforcements include:

- Berries: blueberries, raspberries, blackberries, cranberries, strawberries, fruits,
- Beans: Red beans, kidney beans, pinto and dark beans

- Herbs: oregano, basil, sage, marjoram, thyme, dill, garlic, dry mustard
- Spices: cinnamon, cloves, cumin, turmeric, ginger
- Nuts: walnuts, pecans, pistachios
- Green tea is rich in the two cancer prevention agents and mitigating mixes
- Coffee, cocoa (or dim chocolate) and red wine (yet caffeine and liquor are provocative)
- Exotic organic products: acai, gogi, pomegranate, papaya, pineapple

Eating a greater amount of these mitigating and high cancer prevention agent diet can help lessen incessant inflammation and thusly, decrease your hazard for endless infections. Discover approaches to make these foods a part of your regular diet and you won't just shield your body from illness, yet you may locate that a portion of your a throbbing painfulness improve.

The Anti-Inflammatory Diet for Arthritis Relief

Sustenance and joint inflammation have an association with one another and that is the cause changing your diet is one of the primary recommendations a specialist can give an individual with inflammation in their joints. There are foods that can lessen inflammation and there are those that may intensify the inflammation. An individual with joint pain ought to pursue the anti-inflammatory diet in the event that the person needs to get treated. To begin a mitigating diet, one should know which diet the individual in question going to wipe out in one's diet and which foods will be included.

What is the diet that you ought to maintain a strategic distance from and take out in your diet? With regards to joint inflammation, it is constantly pushed that the individual influenced ought to take out imitation diet like low quality foods, those diet that have been processed and diet with included fake flavorings and colorings. An individual with joint pain ought to likewise maintain a strategic distance from meats that have large amounts of fats and foods that are high in sugar. The reasons why these types of foods ought to be maintained a strategic distance from by individuals with joint pain is that the immersed fats and trans fats found in these types of diet can exacerbate one's condition. The person in question ought to likewise keep away from potatoes, eggplants and tomatoes on the grounds that these are a part of the nightshade group of plant that contains solanine that can incite the pain. Cutting these types of vegetables in individuals with joint pain have not been demonstrated at this point to be viable, however the individuals who pursued this type of diet regularly show enhancements with their condition and discover alleviation from pain.

What is the diet to be included your eating regimen and when you have joint pain? In the event that you definitely know which types of foods you ought to kill in your mitigating diet, you should now realize diet to add to your diet:

1. Solid fats and Oils: Fish oils are high in Omega-3 unsaturated fats that are basic to our wellbeing. This will help reduce the inflammation and keep it from returning. You will likewise get these fats in certain seeds like flaxseed, pumpkin seeds, and sunflower seeds and furthermore in Brazil nuts, almonds, cashew nuts and some more.

2. Foods grown from the ground: You ought to eat more products of the soil and when you have joint inflammation in light of the fact that these have a great deal of mineral, vitamins, cancer prevention agents and photochemical that are advantageous for your joint pain and furthermore to different conditions.

3. Protein: Eating more proteins like fishes and different seafood and poultry meats will likewise help individuals with joint inflammation.

4. Beverages: You should require more fluids to keep your joints greased up. Drink more water, natural product juices, tea, vegetable juice with low sodium and non-fat milk.

Treating yourself for joint pain isn't troublesome and when you know the type of eating diet that is proper for your condition and in the event that you realize the diets to maintain a strategic distance from with joint inflammation just as the foods that must be eaten.

CHAPTER SIX

Dieting Protocol – Meal Plan And Recipes

In this healthy 1,200-calorie supper plan, the standards of a mitigating diet align for seven days of scrumptious, healthy dinners and tidbits, in addition to meal prep tips to set you up for a fruitful week ahead which would take you through a 30-Day venture.

The buzz encompassing inflammation and its association with constant ailments and wellbeing conditions like joint inflammation, diabetes, being overweight, gut issues and coronary illness, may leave you pondering "What is an anti-inflammatory diet?" and "Should I follow it?" A anti-inflammatory diet is tied in with eating a greater amount of the foods that help to fight inflammation in the body, while constraining the foods that will in general increment inflammation, subsequently combatting provocative conditions. The diet accentuates heaps of bright products of the soil, high-fiber vegetables and whole grains, sound fats (like those found in salmon, nuts and olive oil) and cancer prevention agent rich herbs, flavors and tea, while constraining processed diets made with undesirable trans fats, refined starches (like white flour and included sugar) and an excessive amount of sodium.

Since inflammation can be brought about by a lot of different factors other than nourishment, similar to low movement levels, stress and absence of rest, joining solid way of life propensities into your every day schedule can likewise help avert inflammation. To get the most anti-inflammatory advantages, pair this solid dinner plan with standard physical movement (go for 2 1/2 hours of moderate action every week), stress- reducing practices (like yoga, reflection or whatever works best for you), and a decent night's rest each night (at any rate 7 hours out of every night). Regardless of whether you're attempting to effectively reduce inflammation or are just searching for a healthy eating plan, this 7-day anti-inflammatory meal plan can help.

Step by step instructions to Meal-Prep Your Week of Meals:

A little meal prep toward the start of the week will set you up for good dieting achievement.

1. Prep the Vegan Superfood Buddha Bowls to have for lunch on Days 2, 3, 4 and 5. Refrigerate bowls and dressing independently for as long as 4 days. Do not add avocado until prepared to eat to avoid browning.

2. Make the Turmeric-Ginger Tahini Dip to have with snacks consistently.

Day 1

Anti-inflammatory Bonus: Foods high in omega-3 unsaturated fats, for example, salmon, sardines and tuna fish, have been appeared to reduce inflammation levels. Intend to incorporate at any rate two 3-ounce servings of fish high in omega-3 unsaturated fats every week.

Breakfast (287 calories)

- 1 serving Blueberry-Banana Overnight Oats
- 1 cup green tea
- A.M. Bite (31 calories)
- ½ cup blackberries

Lunch (325 calories)

- 1 serving Green Salad with Edamame and Beets

Bite (117 calories)

- 2 Tbsp. Turmeric-Ginger Tahini Dip

- 1 medium carrot, cut into sticks

Supper (442 calories)

- 1 serving Walnut-Rosemary Crusted Salmon
- 1 serving Roasted Squash and Apples with Dried Cherries and Pepitas

Everyday Totals: 1,202 calories, 57 g protein, 131 g starch, 30 g fiber, 54 g fat, 1,520 mg sodium

Day 2

Anti-inflammatory Bonus: Vitamin C, a cancer prevention agent, has mitigating benefits since it helps decline hurtful free extreme cells that may trigger inflammation. Studies demonstrate that individuals who have eats less carbs high in vitamin C have lower levels of the provocative marker C-receptive protein just as lower danger of incendiary infection, similar to gout and coronary illness. The present Raspberry-Kefir Power Smoothie gives forty-five (45%) of the suggested everyday esteem for Vitamin C!

Breakfast (249 calories)

- 1 serving Raspberry-Kefir Power Smoothie

A.M Bite (28 calories)

- 1/3 cup blueberries

Lunch (381 calories)

- 1 serving Vegan Superfood Buddha Bowl

P.M Bite (9 calories)

- ½ cup cut cucumber prepared with a squeeze every one of salt and pepper.

Supper (393 calories)

- 1 serving Indian-Spiced Cauliflower and Chickpea Salad
- 5 ounces unsalted canned tuna fish, in water (depleted)

Top plate of mixed greens with fish.

Night Snack (156 calories)

- 1 ounce dark chocolate

Day by day Totals: 1,215 calories, 70 g protein, 143 g starch, 35 g fiber, 47 g fat, 1,054 mg sodium

Day 3

Anti-inflammatory Bonus: Anthocyanins are ground-breaking cancer prevention agent mixes found in dark blue, red and purple foods grown from the ground, just as red wine. Research demonstrates that anthocyanins assumes the role of reducing inflammation markers, which can decrease danger of malignancy and coronary illness. Keep solidified berries available for an anti-inflammatory lift to your morning smoothies or oats so you can get the advantages notwithstanding when they are not in season.

Breakfast (263 calories)

- 1 cup low-fat plain Greek yogurt
- 1 ½ Tbsp. slashed pecans
- ¼ cup blueberries
- 1 cup green tea

Top yogurt with pecans and blueberries.

A.M Tidbit (42 calories)

- 2/3 cup raspberries

Lunch (381 calories)

- 1 serving Vegan Superfood Buddha Bowl

P.M Tidbit (117 calories)

- 2 Tbsp. Turmeric-Ginger Tahini Dip
- 1 medium carrot, cut into sticks

Supper (409 calories)

- 1 serving Superfood Chopped Salad with Salmon and Creamy Garlic Dressing

Day by day Totals: 1,212 calories 77 g protein, 97 g starch, 28 g fiber, 63 g fat, 813 mg sodium

Day 4

Anti-inflammatory Bonus: Eating dark chocolate and cocoa with some restraint may reduce inflammation markers and improve heart wellbeing. Cocoa is rich in the flavonol quercetin, which is an amazing cancer prevention agent that secures our cells and the reason dark chocolate is a significant part in the anti- inflammatory diet.

Consolidate one 1-ounce square multi day of the darkest chocolate you can discover to boost benefits.

Breakfast (222 calories)

- 1 serving Cocoa-Chia Pudding with Raspberries

A.M Bite (109 calories)

- ½ cup low-fat plain Greek yogurt
- ¼ cup blueberries

Lunch (381 calories)

- 1 serving Vegan Superfood Buddha Bowl

P.M Bite (9 calories)

- ½ cup cut cucumber
- Pinch of salt
- Pinch of pepper

Supper (472 calories)

- 1 serving Stuffed Sweet Potato with Hummus Dressing

Everyday Totals: 1,191 calories, 56 g protein, 168 g sugar, 49 g fiber, 39 g fat, 1,100 mg sodium

Day 5

Anti-inflammatory Bonus: Probiotics, similar to those found in kimchi, yogurt, kefir and fermented tea, help bolster a solid gut. Research demonstrates a sound gut improves our invulnerable mechanisms, keeps up a solid weight and lessens inflammation. Likewise, make sure to likewise incorporate prebiotics, which are unpalatable plant strands found in sustenance like garlic, onions and whole grains that help give fuel to great microbes to upgrade our gut wellbeing.

Breakfast (249 calories)

- 1 serving Raspberry-Kefir Power Smoothie

A.M Bite (2 calories)

- 1 cup green tea

Lunch (381 calories)

- 1 serving Vegan Superfood Buddha Bowl

P.M Bite (58 calories)

- 1 Tbsp. Turmeric-Ginger Tahini Dip
- 3/4 cup cut cucumber

Supper (414 calories)

- 1 serving Korean Steak, Kimchi and Cauliflower Rice Bowl

Night Snack (120 calories)

- 5 ounces red wine

Everyday Totals: 1,224 calories, 57 g protein, 112 g sugar, 28 g fiber, 53 g fat, 1,067 mg sodium

Day 6

Anti-inflammatory Bonus: More than twenty percent (20%) of U.S. grown-ups are influenced by some type of joint pain, which is a provocative disease of the joints, which is regularly treated with a blend of an anti- inflammatory diet and doctor prescribed medicine. The best anti-inflammatory diet routine for joint inflammation incorporates a lot of magnesium— inquire about demonstrates that it reduces inflammation and keeps up joint ligament. Most people don't get enough magnesium, so make sure to incorporate a lot of vegetables, nuts, whole grains, dark green vegetables and seeds to guarantee satisfactory intake.

Breakfast (249 calories)

- 1 serving Raspberry-Kefir Power Smoothie

A.M Tidbit (157 calories)

- 12 pecan parts

Lunch (325 calories)

- 1 serving Green Salad with Edamame and Beets

P.M Tidbit (78 calories)

- 1/2-ounce dim chocolate

Supper (401 calories)

- 1 serving Hummus-Crusted Chicken
- 1 serving Blistered Broccoli with Garlic and Chiles

Food Prep Tip: Cook and hold additional chicken to have with lunch tomorrow. You'll require 2 cups hacked cooked chicken.

Day by day Totals: 1,209 calories, 73 g protein, 94 g starch, 28 g fiber, 63 g fat, 1,245 mg sodium

Day 7

Anti-inflammatory Bonus: An diet high in fiber will have a lower glycemic record, which is a proportion of how foods sway our blood sugars. Fiber is processed gradually, which keeps us full and improves glucose control. A special reward—eating foods lower on the glycemic list may help lessen levels of C-responsive protein, which is a marker for inflammation. This solid mitigating plan takes in any event 28 grams of fiber consistently.

Breakfast (292 calories)

- 1 serving Cocoa-Chia Pudding with Raspberries
- 1 Turmeric Latte

A.M Tidbit (42 calories)

- 1/2 cup blueberries

Lunch (350 calories)

- 1 serving Avocado Egg Salad Sandwiches

P.M Tidbit (116 calories)

- 15 unsalted almonds

Supper (448 calories)

- 1 serving One-Pot Garlicky Shrimp and Spinach
- 1 cup cooked quinoa

Day by day Totals: 1,209 calories, 62 g protein, 128 g sugar, 32 g fiber, 55 g fat, 1,362 mg sodium

Additional Anti-Inflammatory Diet Guidelines

- Drink water and unsweetened coffee and tea. Avoid sodas and other beverages that contain added sugar.
- If you drink alcohol, choose red wine and drink in moderation. A compound present in red wine, resveratrol, has anti-inflammatory properties.
- Satisfy your sweet tooth by choosing dark chocolate in moderation.

What Foods Should I Avoid on an Anti- Inflammatory Diet?

Similarly, as significant as eating more foods that battle inflammation is eating less foods that may cause inflammation. Pursue these rules to free your diet of foods that may build inflammation in your body.

- Avoid profoundly processed foods made with white flour and sugar, similar to white bread and bundled snacks and prepared merchandise.

- Reduce your intake of saturated fat by eating less full-fat dairy, including spread, cream and high-fat cheddar. Greasy meats contain high measures of saturated fat, as do items made with palm oil and coconut oil.

- Cut back on animal proteins, including red meat, cheddar and yogurt. Concentrate your protein intake on omega-3-rich fish and plant sources.

Conclusion

An anti-inflammatory diet was not created in light of weight reduction, yet all things considered, eating a diet high in some low-calorie, supplement rich foods, similar to natural products, vegetables and beans, and low in processed foods and included sugars, will prompt weight reduction. One thing to note is that albeit high-fat sustenance like avocados and nuts are gainful, they are additionally high in calories. Be aware of your amounts when choosing these diets.

Considering these certainties, it's critical to realize that an anti-inflammatory diet has not been demonstrated to battle inflammation related ailments, however the foods and dietary patterns diet elevates, have been appeared to have many medical advantages.

In general, an anti-inflammatory diet is a sound method for eating that is in accordance with food standards. This diet advances what we've been discussing: a sound diet incorporates organic products, vegetables, whole grains, and solid fats. Limiting processed, browned, refined, sugary diets is a smart idea for a more beneficial diet, as a lot of those kinds of foods may prompt the advancement of perpetual ailments. Following this diet should expand your vitamin, mineral, and fiber intake and will probably make you feel more useful and perhaps help you shed pounds.

Made in the USA
San Bernardino, CA
04 August 2020